About the Book

"No human goal is more important than that of realizing the potential for self-actualization and achieving it. *Unlimited Futures* gives you all of the tools you need to reach your goals."
> — C. Norman Shealy, M.D., Ph.D., founder, Shealy Wellness Center; founding president, American Holistic Medical Association, and author of twenty-six books and numerous scientific papers.

"Discover your true purpose in life and how to fulfill it. Become a self-actualized human being with *Unlimited Futures*. This book is a powerful and practical guide to personal transformation. Read it and leap!"
> —Chef Jerry Bartholow, author, *Peace Soup—The recipe for a peaceful life in the new millennium.*

"Dr. Stevens brings us a fresh and illuminating approach to self-mastery. She uncovers specific laws of nature that govern our lives and gives us step-by-step guidelines for discovering how to live in harmony with them."
> —Jack Canfield, co-author, *Chicken Soup for the Soul.*

"*Unlimited Futures* is a complete and compelling source for anyone who is interested in developing a higher, more fulfilling and purposeful life. Dr. Bobbie Stevens writes in an easy-to-read style, including many examples and practical exercises. This book reflects her insight and talent in teaching others how to manifest goals and desires in keeping with spiritual principles. I highly recommend *Unlimited Futures* as a valuable guide."
> —Jack Kern, minister

"*With Unlimited Futures,* Bobbie Stevens creates a design for creating a higher spiritual awareness."
> —James Redfield, author of *Celestine Prophecy: The Secret of Shambhala.*

"*Unlimited Futures* is a compilation of Dr. Stevens's lifelong experience developing the philosophy and techniques that she teaches in the courses which she and her husband, Dr. Dean Portinga, have given to thousands of fortunate people. Incorporating diverse elements of psychology and philosophy, she has created a pragmatic approach that is now presented in very understandable terms for everyone. As I read this thorough text, I reexperienced the course that I took with them some years ago. I would encourage anyone who wants their life to be more fulfilling to read this book over and over."
> —Steven Hollenbeck, M.D., family physician

"Through research and discovery, Bobbie Stevens has developed a seven-step process for creating an ideal life. This process has changed my life! *Unlimited Futures* gives step-by-step instructions and examples so you, too, can enjoy an ideal life. The information in this book is priceless!"

> —Joan E. Gustafson, president, Success and Leadership Dynamics; author, *A Woman Can Do That!: 10 Strategies for Creating Success in Your Life.*

"Our beliefs, accumulated over a lifetime, often get in the way of our possibilities. Bobbie and the *Unlimited Futures* course has helped me, my wife, my employees and many others to release the power that we all have within us to give our gifts to the world, to our loved ones, and to ourselves."

> — John Christensen, CEO, ChartHouse Learning, co-author, *Fish*

"Unlimited Futures is a book that will inspire and stimulate you to reach your potential. I have been a practicing doctor of chiropractic for over fifty years, and this book gave me the warm fuzzies. Highly recommended to all!"

> —C. R. Gustafson, D.C.

"Bobbie Stevens has managed to map out a road to higher consciousness that not only inspires us as to where we can go, but most importantly, how we can get there. Her specific practices for turning these grand ideas into directed action will empower and energize anyone who is serious about experiencing the frontiers of personal potential."

> —William G. VanArsdale, executive producer, "Inner Voyages," TV series

What course participants say about the Unlimited Futures Course

"The Unlimited Futures course is life-changing. No longer do you react to life, you take charge of creating your ideal life with powerful new insights and tools to do so! There is an immense awakening regarding who you are, how you function and why you are here. Everything in your experience is wonderfully transformed, enhanced and changed on every level through this new expanded awareness. This knowledge and these skills absolutely bring my life greater peace, joy and meaning as it continues to unfold perfectly according to my vision. I am so very, very grateful for this exquisite experience."

—Cheryl O'Shaughnessy, business owner

"I have just completed the Unlimited Futures course for the seventh time. Why do I keep repeating it? Because each time I reach a higher level of understanding or unfoldment. The Unlimited Futures course is so powerful because it is holistic psychology instead of secular. My friend the late Dr. Robert Hobert (industrial psychologist) observed that all effective executive development programs are spiritual development programs. I have come to call this program the Miracles Process because, to my knowledge, there is no other program in the world that has the power this process has for developing an individual's ability to create whatever he/she chooses. It truly is a miracle."

—Thomas E. Clague, consultant/coach

"I have had two severe heart attacks; the last one was two months before I was introduced to the Unlimited Futures course. Without this course I would probably not be alive today. I have gained more and more, better and better health, ever since I began my first program with Unlimited Futures fifteen years ago. My focus was on my health and it has improved beyond my ability to imagine before this course. I now focus on whatever I want, and I easily see golden opportunities."

—Robert M. Cargill, retired grain executive

"I have found that the principles and practices from the Unlimited Futures program allow me to deal with normally stressful situations in a calm and effective manner. I believe anyone would find it to be a growth experience that would adapt to their specific needs."

—Ken Larson, CEO, Polaris Industries, Inc.

"EXCELLENT! By far the best personal development program I have ever experienced."
    —Jim Swindal, director of Engineering, Tora Company

"My participation in the Unlimited Futures core course has helped me to make some very important changes in my life externally, and more importantly to me, internally. The simple fact that I actually know what my ambitions and desires are automatically brings some stability and contentment to my life. But watching those desires become fulfilled is an inspiring experience, and I have just scratched the surface."
    —Michael Johnson, recording artist

"Profoundly powerful and hard to describe. The best thing I have experienced in forty-five years. Puts consulting in a very different realm."
    —Patrick Powers, Ph.D. business consultant

"Areas of my life that I felt were good before and really didn't need improvement, have become great. Personal relationships are stronger and more open than ever before. Prior to the course, I viewed my job as low stress; however, it would take forty-five to fifty hours a week to accomplish what needed to be done. During the course I discovered my body was holding a large amount of stress, and my beliefs about my job were not correct. After completing the course . . . I have minimized my time at work and increased my productivity."
    —Glenn Myers, vice president, Giefer Sales Company

"Once the stress was released by doing the exercises in the course, many, many exciting events happened. Life turned joyful, my vision of the future became very clear. Learning that what is going to happen will come totally from inside me is a wonderful life learning experience."
    — Michael Ketcham, business owner

"I learned that the energizers are so important in order to open up the energy flow. I learned to relax more and let things happen without getting stressed. I love this course. I have taken it four times and could keep taking it because every time I get something different."
    —Jean Ketcham, business owner

"The greatest gift in life is to remain in fully recognized and realized connection to your source. In this course and the continued practice of this program you can, in fact, establish this and become an unfolding picture of all your dreams."
    —Ronald W. Jensen, psychologist/minister

"The course is a complete process for creating anything I desire in my life. I have learned to really expand my vision of what is possible and how to move through any obstacles I think exist."
—Mary Jo Walter, accountant

"Dear Bobbie and Dean:
Thank you.
For showing me the way to open my life and accept all that awaits me.
For showing me how to laugh at the external forces that attempt to limit me.
For showing me that no matter what my vision may be, it is important.
For showing me that I am Love."
—Janet L. Vrevig, business woman

"The Unlimited Futures course is extraordinary. It has brought me to a new level of goal achievement, enjoyment of life, focus on purpose, and abundance in all ways. Through living the seven steps in the creative process I am well on my way to creating a life of choice rather than chance."
—Tara Tuck, president, Tara Publishing

"WOW! What a life changer the Unlimited Futures course has been for me. It has brought a better and working understanding of the many self-help books I have read. I understood the ideas, but taking the Unlimited Futures course has enabled me to implement the ideas in a practical way with tangible results. It is difficult for me to imagine anyone taking this course seriously and not coming away a changed person. Thank you for making such an enriching experience available. In gratitude,"
—Landon Kite, Jr., CEO Quantum Management Associates, Inc.

"The opportunity to join this 'creative process course' came at a time of unprecedented stress in my life. It provided me support equal to the stress by means of new knowledge, practical methods and a framework for what I knew already and what I will come to know. In the end I learned how to create the life I want. As a physician, trained in the sciences, the connection to quantum physics was most helpful. With the five basic choices I now move through life with much greater awareness and intentionality than before. I am a helper who is now more adept at giving help and receiving help."
—Milton H. Seifert Jr., M.D., family physician

A Word about the Unlimited Futures Executive Development Program

"In my personal view, these are some of the most important attributes of good leaders:

- good judgment and decisiveness
- creativity and intuitive insight
- vision for the enterprise
- ethics and responsible choices
- motivation of self and others
- effective interpersonal relationships
- creation of team spirit and high morale

Leadership traits are in turn dependent upon more fundamental capabilities:

- improving stress management
- quieting the mind
- increasing focus and concentration
- accessing intuitive awareness
- uncovering and replacing self-limiting beliefs
- discovering our personal vision and mission

These underlying capabilities are strengthened through the Unlimited Futures Executive Development Program, so that leadership traits become second nature. The corporation gains a much more effective leader, while the individual becomes more successful and finds greater enjoyment in success."

—Alan Norton, director, 3M Corporation

Unlimited
Futures

Unlimited
Futures

How to Understand the Life You Have
and
Create the Life You Want

Bobbie R. Stevens, PH.D.

Tara Publishing

ISBN: 0-9706497-0-3
Library of Congress Control Number: 2001-131322
Cover design: OspreyDesign
Typesetting and design: Tabby House

Publishers Cataloging in Publication
(provided by Quality Books, Inc.)

Stevens, Bobbie R.
    Unlimited futures : how to understand the life you
have and create the life you want / Bobbie R. Stevens.
– 1st ed.
    p. cm.
    includes index.
    LCCN: 2001-131322
    ISBN: 0-9706497-0-3

    1. Self-actualization (Psychology) 2. Motivation
(Psychology) I. Title.

BF637.S4S74 2001   158.1
                        QBI101-200203

Tara Publishing
3823 Tamiami Trail #232
Naples, FL 34112
1-866-563-1493
941-513-4029 (local)

Dedication

To Dean Portinga
My best friend, husband and business partner
and
To all Unlimited Futures course participants.

Contents

Part Four: From Caterpillars to Butterflies

Foreword

Bobbie Stevens gives us a comprehensive view of how life works, combining age-old wisdom with current knowledge in becoming a self-actualized person. *Unlimited Futures* lays out a clear path to transformation with practical methods and techniques for creating the lives we want in a better world.

The book teaches the principles of a higher order and inspires us to commit to our soul's purpose. With personal anecdotes and information from great minds, Dr. Stevens explains how to eliminate self-defeating habits in expanding our physical, mental, and spiritual creative potential.

Unlimited Futures is a book to keep close at hand, to read, study, remind, and practice its steps for manifesting the self you were meant to be.

—Jane Kern, Ph.D.
Educational Leadership Consultant and author
of *Inventing a School: Expanding the Boundaries of Learning*

Acknowledgments

First, I would like to thank all the people who have participated in the Unlimited Futures courses over the years. Thanks for sharing your lives with us, and giving me the opportunity to test and prove over and over again the value of this program. Also, thanks for all of your support in helping us to spread the word of the great possibilities that are available for all of us.

I want to express my sincere appreciation to Jane Kern for her support and for introducing me to the Maui Writers Retreat. Also a special thanks to Bud Gardner, Dan Poynter and Jack Canfield for their help at the retreat and beyond.

Thanks to the women in our community book club for your support, and especially to Inace Dobberteen for organizing the club and supplying me with materials about writing that I needed.

A very special feeling of appreciation and gratitude goes to the people who read my book and had the kind words to say about it that you just read. These people are Jack Canfield, James Redfield, Dr. Norman Shealy, Joan and Cliff Gustafson, John Christensen, Jack and Jane Kern, Dr. Steven Hollenbeck, Jerry and Jane Bartholow and Bill VanArsdale.

I also want to acknowledge our many friends and business associates who were very helpful in giving me feedback on the book. These include my editor Tara Tuck, Landon Kite, Bob and Gail Johnston, Mike, Michelle and Jean Ketchum, and Art and Dotti Holt.

A special thanks also goes to the course participants whose testimonials I have used to give you an overview of what people say about the Unlimited Futures courses. They are:

Cheryl O'Shaughnessy, Tom Clague, Bob Cargill, Ken Larson, Jim Swindal, Michael Johnson, Pat Powers, Glenn Myers, Mike Ketcham, Jean Ketcham, Ron Jensen, Mary Jo Walter, Jan Vrevig, Tara Tuck, Landon Kite, and Milt Seifert. Also thanks to Al Norton for his assessment of our Executive Development Program.

Last, but not least, I want to express my appreciation to my husband, Dean Portinga, who always supports me fully in whatever I choose to do.

Introduction

*The ills from which we are suffering have had their seat in
the very foundation of human thought. But today
something is happening to the whole structure of human
consciousness. A fresh kind of life is starting. There is for
us in the future not only survival, but superlife.*—Teilhard
de Chardin, *The Phenomenon of Man*

Unlimited Futures is about the "superlife." What would the
superlife be like? Have you ever wondered what your life would
be like if you were totally in charge and could create every aspect of your life just the way you would like it to be? What would
you create?

Most of us would probably start with health. We would want
to be perfectly healthy, full of energy and vitality. Our minds
would be clear and sharp. We might even be brilliant or, at least,
highly intelligent. We would probably look good and have a pleas-
ant personality. The people in our lives would respect and love
us. All of our relationships would be happy and harmonious,
and we would create a loving intimate relationship with a very
special person. We would create a career that provided interesting, fulfilling work, which would allow us to use our many talents. Then we would be sure we had all the money we needed to
buy all the material things we wanted in our lives, like a beautiful place to live, great clothes and luxury transportation. This
would be a good start, right?

Even though most of us could agree that we would like these things, if we each created them for our own lives, each life would still be very different. What these general statements mean to me would be very different from what they would mean to you, and they would look very different in each of our lives. By now you are probably saying, "What's the point? Let's get real. I have the life I have and I don't know how to change it. Things just happen. I don't know why. I just do the best I can."

Many years ago when I first started college, I began to wonder why some people are so much more successful than others in all areas of life. What is the key to happiness, fulfillment, wealth? People I asked about this told me things such as, "It's hard work," "high IQ," "connections," "luck."

As I looked more carefully at these assumptions, they all proved incorrect. I knew some people who worked hard and gained some degree of success, but there were others who worked hard and showed little or no success. I knew people with high IQs who were successful in some areas of life, and others with high IQs who were leading very disappointing lives. The same proved to be true with connections. Since none of us know exactly what luck is, it is hard to rule it out; however, it doesn't seem to offer much help in understanding the question.

I knew there had to be an answer to my question. It seemed to me that this was a huge gap in human knowledge, and I was determined to find out what was responsible for the choices we make and the resulting experiences.

Since my major was psychology, I eventually found the works of Abraham Maslow. Maslow was the first psychologist to study psychologically healthy people. Before Maslow's studies, published in the 1960s, the entire field of psychology was based on the study of psychologically sick people.

Maslow noticed that there were some people who functioned on a totally different level than most of the other people he knew. He decided to study these people to discover what made them different. These very healthy people saw the world from a totally different perspective. They were highly intuitive.

They had the ability to know things from a source that others were not able to access. They saw beauty and order, and experienced life from a different dimension than other people. Maslow said they lived peaceful, joyous lives and made significant contributions to the world. He coined the term "self-actualized" to describe the way these people functioned.

Maslow reported that these self-actualized people had transcended needs. They had discovered the ability within themselves to fulfill their needs and desires.

Maslow's observations could be the answer to my question. If some people lived from this more advanced level, then it must be a human potential. Maslow observed that the people who lived on this advanced plane were different, and gave us some great insights into a new level of functioning through his study of these self-actualized people.

My next question was "How does one become self-actualized?" It seems that some people are simply born with these abilities. However, I knew that these must be innate abilities that could be developed. My hope was to discover how we all can develop these abilities within ourselves. For many years I looked for the answer, but didn't find a clue.

Then in 1968 I discovered the answer to my question. It seemed to be quite by accident, but now I know it was not by accident at all. I began an experiment to discover a way to quit smoking, but I discovered much, much more. I discovered a process for developing self-actualization.

In the first part of this book I share with you my experiment, and how it worked for me. After many years of experimenting with this process and proving its validity over and over again, I designed a program to help others develop their potential. I then founded Unlimited Futures, a company that provides this program. Thousands of people have attended these Unlimited Futures courses over the years, with outstanding results. I will share some of their experiences with you. What we discovered is that self-actualization is an automatic result of high-level health or wellness.

In Part Two we explore what self-actualization is. We look at the characteristics that Maslow found in the self-actualized people he studied. We also discover why we are not all self-actualized. We look at some basic laws of nature that govern our lives. They are laws that are affecting us all the time, such as gravity. Once we understand how these laws are working in our lives, we can then see how and why we experience the things we do and how we create our own experiences. We explore how choice works, and who gets to make the choices. We learn how to create optimal health and live in harmony with the laws of nature that govern our lives.

In Part Three, we compare how the ordinary person perceives and handles life's situations with how the self-actualized person responds. We look at situations in one's personal life, relationship situations, and the differences in how the ordinary person and the self-actualized person each function in the workplace. Then in the last chapter of Part Three we project how society will change as more people become self-actualized.

In Part Four we lay out a process that will bring us to higher levels of health, wellness and self-actualization. It is a process that takes place over time. We are all looking for a quick fix, but to my knowledge there isn't one. The beauty of this process or lifestyle is that one's health and life continues to get better and better. We discover that we really can take charge of our lives and create the kind of life we have always longed for.

Just reading this book will not change your life unless you choose to make the commitment necessary to follow the guidelines and experience the results for yourself. No one else can do it for us. It doesn't matter how many books we read, how many tapes we listen to, or how many courses we attend—it is all just information until we choose to implement it into our own lives.

We all have certain things that we do regularly as a result of our beliefs. When we sum up these habits and actions, this forms what we call our lifestyle. All of us have created lifestyles that we believe are what we need to be doing to create the life we want. However, as we look at the laws that govern our life experiences, we may realize that we need to make some changes. No matter what our experiences are or what our physical condition is at the present time, we just start from where we are, do whatever is possible for us to do in following the guidelines in Part Four, and watch a transformation take place in our lives.

An example of a transformation is seen in the process of a caterpillar becoming a butterfly. The world of a caterpillar and the world of a butterfly are very different realities. The caterpillar is wormlike as it struggles along trying to feed itself and survive in a very small world, usually just a few yards of space.

The butterfly, on the other hand, can fly. Its world is very large. Butterflies can fly thousands of miles and some even travel internationally. The butterfly's world is one of freedom and ease. Butterflies do not need to struggle to find food. They feed from the sweet nectar of the flowers just for the taking. They fulfill their purpose of bringing beauty to the world easily, by being themselves and carrying pollen from flower to flower. Simply being who they are fulfills their purpose.

Every caterpillar has the potential to become a butterfly.

A butterfly is a mature caterpillar. The caterpillar, in its immaturity or undiscovered potential, struggles along doing the best it knows how to fulfill its needs in this state. However, in the process it damages crops and is considered a nuisance. Consequently most caterpillars never reach their full potential. Once they reach their full potential, by becoming butterflies, they are able to fulfill all their needs without harming anything. They live a life of freedom, ease and abundance as they fulfill their purpose, and make their contribution to the world.

This much-expanded reality is the result of a transformation process that is necessary for the caterpillar to fulfill its potential and become a butterfly.

This is a parallel analogy to what we as people experience in discovering who we are, and actualizing our potential. This book is about understanding how you can go through your own transformation process. The process itself, just as with the caterpillar, is an internal process.

People do not look as drastically different outwardly as do butterflies from caterpillars, but as this inner process takes place in our thoughts, beliefs, actions and experiences it is certainly no less spectacular than that of the caterpillar. We, too, create a much-expanded reality for ourselves. We discover a whole new world. Within each of us lies the potential to expand our horizons, fulfill our needs, create the life we want for ourselves, fulfill our purpose and make a wonderful contribution to the world. We, too, just like butterflies, can live lives of freedom, ease and abundance.

This book is about you—who you are, how you function, your purpose and how to accomplish it.

My purpose in writing this book is to share this knowledge and provide step-by-step guidelines that all can follow for creating a lifestyle that will bring the greatest possible health, happiness, love and fulfillment into their lives. I write this with the deepest gratitude for the revelation to me of this knowledge, and the wonderful opportunity to share it with you. May you be as abundantly blessed as I have been.

And as a final note, I would like to challenge someone to come up with a new pronoun that means *either* male or female. I tried to use "they," but "they" told me that it was not grammatically correct when speaking of just one person. This left me with no alternative but to follow what writers have done in the past—to use the pronoun "he" to mean both male and female. We need a new word. In fact we need a number of new words, and this is a good place to start. If you find your purpose is to help clarify our language, please accept this challenge.

Part One

Breaking the Limits

My Search for the Meaning of Life and Discovery of a Whole New World

No barriers, masses of matter however enormous, can withstand the powers of the mind; the remotest corners yield to them; all things succumb; the very Heaven itself is laid open.—Marcus Manilius, Roman author, c. 40 B.C.

The year was 1968 and I was living alone for the second time in my life. My first experience was not a good one. I was very lonely and not at all prepared for having that much time to myself. This time I was determined to make it work. It was the perfect time to take stock of my life.

I am an only child, but always had many friends to keep me company. My parents owned several small businesses, which I worked in as I was growing up. I got married right out of high school, and started my work career. My better judgment told me to go to college, but all of my friends were getting married. It just seemed to be the thing to do.

I got married mostly to keep from hurting my boyfriend, which seems ridiculous now, but at the time I didn't know what else to do. We had very little in common, and the marriage ended in divorce four years later. I felt sad, of course, but mostly I felt a great sense of freedom. Now I could choose who I wanted to be, the career I wanted to pursue, and a whole new life for myself. Then came the question: "What do I want to do with my life?" There were so many things to think about; so many possible choices I could make.

3

I was very much interested in business, and was, at the time, going to business school at night. After getting my degree in accounting, I seriously considered taking the exam to become a CPA, but soon realized that I was much more interested in working with people than numbers.

I had often wondered why some people are so successful while others fail. I heard all the different theories floating around. Some people believed it was education—if you get a good education you will be successful. Others said you needed a high IQ. Neither theory seemed plausible to me. I knew people who were highly educated yet were not what I would consider successful. Others belonged to MENSA, but couldn't even get a job. There had to be something else, and I wanted to know why some people are so much more successful than others in all areas. It also seemed to me that most problems in life were related to the way we think. This discovery sent me back to school to study psychology.

College was fun for me even though I worked full time. The study of psychology, however, was not what I had hoped it would be. Our study was mostly in the field of abnormal psychology, but my interest was in the field of possibilities. I wanted to know what was different about people who lead happy, successful lives and made significant contributions to the world. After a few years in the study of psychology, it became obvious that I would not be learning the answers to my questions there. It was time to rethink the direction of my life. There had to be something more fun to do than study abnormal psychology.

Modeling school sounded like fun. I decided to try it, and it was indeed fun. Our teacher had us listen to and work with a recording by Earl Nightingale, which gave us instructions for creating whatever we wanted. We were to set our goals, write them down and look at them every day. Then we were to act upon whatever came to us to fulfill our goals. She said we should experiment with this technique, and that we really could accomplish our goals, whatever they were.

Our teacher believed there were only two career choices that made sense for women at that time, either modeling or becoming an airline stewardess (as it was called in those days). Traveling appealed to me, and so did the idea of meeting lots of interesting people. Since I was too short to be taken very seriously as a fashion model outside the petite arena, I decided to become an airline stewardess. I followed Nightingale's instructions and did accomplish all of my goals, including landing a job as a stewardess with a major airline. I felt pretty good about this since I was told they hired only one out of one hundred interviewed at that time. I vowed to continue using this procedure, but soon forgot it in the busy time of moving and starting my new career. I met many interesting people and enjoyed visiting places I had never seen before.

We worked about eighty hours a month which gave me time to take some classes and stay involved in the business world.

Now, in 1968, I had been with the airlines for eight years and had traveled around the world. It was time to take a serious look at my life. In the past, I usually had two or three jobs or major projects going at the same time. I also had an active social life, but there was something missing. I decided to take some time to be alone and ask some important questions—questions such as: "What is life really all about?" "Why am I here?" and "What should I be doing with my life?" It seemed to me that there had to be more to life than what I, and everyone I knew, understood. The meaning and purpose of life had to be more than mere survival and consumption of goods and services.

That feeling of loneliness or emptiness inside continued to persist. Most of us think that loneliness can be eliminated by having someone special in our lives, but I knew that was not the answer. I had been in several very special relationships, even though I was not in a special relationship at this time. I knew that if I stayed busy enough with my relationships and my work, I wouldn't have time to think about the important questions. This was not a time for another relationship; it was a time for my own personal growth.

There was so much I didn't understand—things that I truly wanted to know, like why things go so well at times then fall apart at others. What is luck? Where does it come from and why? What role do we each play in creating our experiences, and how does it work? As I was thinking on these things one day, I saw an article in a magazine about some breathing exercises that were supposed to help people quit smoking. I had started smoking after becoming a flight attendant. At that time cigarettes were served on every tray, and smoking was the "in" thing to do. All of my roommates smoked, and I joined them, but I always hated the fact that I had become addicted.

I had quit smoking many times, and once even made it for eight months. Then a crisis arose and I started again. Even when I had been able to give up smoking for almost a year, I still wanted a cigarette every time I saw someone else smoking. When I would start smoking again I would always smoke more than before. It was definitely compulsive behavior. It was as if I had to make up for the time I had lost when not smoking, as if I had a goal to smoke a certain number of cigarettes. I never became involved with drugs, but from listening to others' experiences, it seems very much the same. Now was the time to rid myself of this addiction.

I found a teacher to help me with the breathing exercises that I had read about. She also taught me some stretching exercises. Within the next few weeks, while looking for a book on stretching exercises, I found a book on focusing techniques and meditation. I put together a routine of all these things and started doing it daily. I decided to quit smoking again a few days after I started my breathing lessons. This time it was different; I had no desire to smoke again. Within a few weeks I began to feel more energetic and my mind seemed to become sharper. I thought it was just the result of freeing my body of the tar and nicotine I had been feeding it each day, and I am sure that was a major factor in the beginning.

However, within a few months I began to experience a continued increase in energy. I felt younger and more confident. In fact, my energy level was more like that of a sixteen-year-old than that of a thirty-three-year-old person. Along with this increase of energy came a very calm and peaceful feeling. I felt quite whole and complete. This was something that I had never felt before. The loneliness I had felt in the past had completely gone. In fact, I loved being alone. I was growing by leaps and bounds. I practiced my routine of breathing exercises, stretching exercises, meditation and focusing techniques daily. I felt so great, I even decided to set aside one day a month for being totally alone. I wouldn't even answer the phone. It was a day of silence for me, where I would practice my routine, experiment and read.

As time went on, I started having very strong feelings of love. I had been in love with someone close to me several times and, of course, I loved my family. But this was different. I was in love with life. Everything seemed lighter, and I felt an inner joy. I was truly happy, and this happiness didn't relate to anyone or anything outside myself. I was not unhappy before, but this was a totally new experience for me. Somehow I wanted to express this love, and since it wasn't related to anyone in particular, it seemed to express itself through greater kindness and thoughtfulness for everyone I met. There were times when the love seemed so strong that in my mind I would simply bless people whom I had never seen before. Somehow I knew that we are all connected, and if I thought of blessing them that they would indeed be blessed.

This was a very different experience from the fast-paced, results-oriented, bottom line, get-to-the-point-and-move-on kind of person that I had always been. Life was taking on a whole new meaning for me.

I had probably been practicing my routine each day for about a year when I started noticing that I would know something was going to happen before it actually occurred. Many times the phone would ring and I would know who was calling before I answered it. At first this was simply fascinating, then I realized that if I could know these things automatically, maybe I could get answers to my questions. I began experimenting with this possibility—and it worked.

My experiment started with questions that I could find the answers to, or at least ones that I knew had answers. After finishing my routine, while I was still in a very quiet place, I would ask a question. Then I would listen for the answer to come into my consciousness. Sometimes an answer would come; other times the answer didn't come right away, but I knew it would eventually. Usually within days, sometimes weeks, the answers to my questions would show up. They came in numerous ways. Sometimes the answer simply appeared in my consciousness, then sometimes I would pick up a book and find it there. Other times it would show up on TV, or someone would tell me the answer I was seeking. It was a most interesting experiment to notice how I always got answers, even though they came in various ways. I checked them out and found them to be true.

I had many, many questions about life and how it worked. I truly wanted to understand how experiences are created, why things happen as they do, and who or what is responsible. These were questions that to my knowledge did not have answers, or at least not answers that I could accept as true. After experimenting with questions that I could verify for some months, I decided it was time to ask these more important questions. This experiment started with the question, "What role do we each play in creating our own experiences?" At that moment the answer started to unfold, or appear in my consciousness. This unfoldment continued on for several months. It simply came to me and I knew that I knew; there was no doubt in my mind.

I could see that everything in existence is made of energy, and that energy is moved and directed and formed by intelligence, and that intelligence is based in love. The love that I was experiencing was not about something external, this love was who we all are. I could see that Love is the power source of the universe. Love contains all intelligence and is the source of all energy. On a conscious level I was experiencing what Einstein referred to as the unified field. I could see that everything in the universe originates from the same source. This source, which we access through silence or stillness, described by physicists as absolute zero, is all there is.

When Love—the source—moves, energy is created. This energy is moved in an intelligent way to create all of existence. Consequently, everyone and everything is this Love, Intelligence and Energy. We are all this oneness. Our separateness is only in form. I could clearly see that we live in a perfect universe, and there are nonchanging laws of nature or principles of life that are responsible for how it works. I began to perceive these principles and understand how they worked. It was quite clear to see that given this understanding, I could create anything I wanted.

One of these principles is that **mental energy directs physical energy.**

This is how we create the experiences in our lives. We create our own experiences through our own thoughts, or more accurately, through our deepest beliefs. Once I knew this I could clearly see how my friends and I had created our experiences. It was really very funny, because it is so simple once we understand it. On the other hand, it was quite sad to see what we do to ourselves simply because we do not understand the laws of nature or principles of life that we are each using every day. It is like trying to play a game without knowing the rules.

It was clear to see that **our beliefs are simply information that we have accepted as truth.** Many of our beliefs have simply been programed into our consciousness from our environment. Some have been handed down from generation to generation and many more are beliefs that have been accepted by our society as truth, and we have never even questioned them. It is a vicious circle; we have a belief about something that creates that experience, which in turn validates the belief. This is how we keep creating the same kind of experiences for ourselves. The tricky part about beliefs is that about eighty-five percent of what we believe is not on the conscious level. We don't know what we believe until we bring it into our consciousness.

The knowledge that beliefs are simply information that we have accepted as truth, and that we can change them to create what we want rather than what we don't want, was a great relief. I realized that I believed many things that were not helping me to create the life I wanted. This started the next phase of my growth. I could see that **the choices we make create our experiences** and those choices are governed by our beliefs. There are truly infinite possibilities, but they are guided by the information that we accept as truth. My next project was to become aware of the many beliefs I had that were not useful to me, and to change them. This concept was not new, but, until now, I had no idea about how to actually change a belief.

After concentrated focus on changing my beliefs for about a month, I was now ready to start working with creating. After all, it was most exciting to know that I could create anything I wanted. The next question, of course, was what would I want to create? I gave this serious thought. Where should I start? I could see that there was a process for creating anything. First I needed to decide what I wanted to create, then I needed to visualize it as being a part of my life. This visualization creates a form for the energy to move into. The third step was acceptance. This is where our beliefs come in. If I could not believe in my desire and fully accept it, the energy for its fulfillment would be repelled. Fortunately for me at that time, I was totally prepared. I could see how the process worked, and was strong and clear enough to work with it. The fourth step was to focus my attention on it. Then I needed to listen for guidance. I knew that I would intuitively know what I needed to do. I simply needed to follow through with the action and my creation would materialize. It was now time to start my first creation after understanding how the process works.

The first question was what did I want? I wanted to create something on a very material level so I could easily see how the process worked and that it did indeed work. I wanted to experience how these principles would work in a business situation. I decided that what I wanted to create on a material level was my own place to live. I was single and living alone in an apartment. I didn't want the upkeep of a house; what I wanted was a townhouse. One of the immediate problems was that there weren't any townhouses in my area. Townhouses were new at the time. I had seen them in other parts of the country, but there weren't any in Minnesota. I knew this didn't matter, it would just make the process more interesting. Once I knew what I wanted to create, I needed to clearly visualize it in my mind in as much detail as possible. I visited townhouses in other cities and got a clear image in my mind of what mine would look like. Not only did I see the number of rooms, their location and sizes, but I also bought furniture in my mind, including a grand piano, and decorated the townhouse the way I wanted it to be.

I wanted this vision to be as big as I could imagine, something that I was not capable of accomplishing if I had to do things the way I had in the past. I decided that in addition to the new townhouse for myself, I should also create a second townhouse to rent out for additional income. Then I decided I should have a new car to go in my new garage, which, of course, I visualized in detail. This was as much as I could imagine at this time. The next step was acceptance. Could I accept all of this in my life now? I had already changed my beliefs to correspond with the new understanding that I now had—that **beliefs are only information that we have accepted**. I knew, without a shadow of a doubt, that my vision would manifest and that it would all happen within a year.

My next step was to keep my attention focused on the vision until it actually manifested in the material world. Next I became quiet and still, and asked what I should do to help this vision manifest. It came to me that I should get a real estate license. I followed through, studied the books, took the test and got a real estate license. What next? Then came the idea that I should get a job selling real estate. Well, I didn't see how this would help, since there weren't any townhouses, but I followed my guidance, and began reading the want ads in the paper by real estate companies looking for agents. I came across one that caught my attention—it invited people to take a test to see if they would be successful in real estate. I applied, took a battery of tests that took about three hours to complete, and was hired.

After about three weeks my boss called me into his office and told me my test results had arrived from the firm that had analyzed them. I asked if it showed that I would be successful in real estate. He said, yes, I would most likely be successful, but he was very concerned about one of the answers I had given on my test. I immediately knew what he was talking about. One of the questions on the test asked how much money you expect to

11

make your first year in real estate. Well, I had already figured out how much money I would need to buy both my townhouses, furnish the one I planned to live in the way I wanted, and buy my new car, so I entered that figure as the answer to that question. I knew they would be concerned about my expectation, but I decided to put it down anyway. He looked at me for a few minutes then asked, "Do you know how many houses you would have to sell to make that much money?" I said, "No." It was a good thing that I hadn't figured that out, or I might have doubted, which would have repelled the energy necessary to fulfill my vision. He informed me that it took him five years of very hard work to make that much money. I finally convinced him that I wasn't crazy, but I told him that was my vision and that I would keep working toward it.

To make a long story short, I made exactly the amount I had written on the form my first year in real estate. However, I was with that company only about three months when one of the agents told me about an apartment complex that was being converted into townhouses to be sold individually. I went over to take a look, and met the developer who was doing the conversion. I asked him if he had ever thought about building new townhouses. He said he had, and was in the process of putting together his plans for a new development at that time. He told me about it, but it didn't sound like what I had in mind. I had clearly seen in my mind's eye the location, size and surroundings of the townhouse development I wanted to be in. I shared my vision with him and asked if he would consider looking for the land and building what I had envisioned. He said he was always open to new possibilities. Immediately I knew things were coming together. I told him that I would sell the units in that location if he would build the development I had described to him. He was impressed with my confidence that I could sell his units. We decided to work together and my vision began to have tangible results.

That particular conversion didn't work out due to some problems with code and structure, but he bought another apartment complex which we were able to convert into townhouses.

I bought a townhouse in that development, decorated it, and moved in. I used it for a model until we could get the models ready. It was clear to me that this would be my rental townhouse. Only a few weeks had passed when he called me and said he had a phone call from a man who owned a piece of land used as a nursery, which was located in a residential area. He thought it sounded very much like what I had described to him. We looked at it, and it was exactly what I had seen in my mind's eye. The size was perfect, and it had beautiful mature trees lining the entire property. It was located about ten minutes from the airport on a very beautiful residential street. This was it; my vision was manifesting.

He bought an option to buy the land. The next step was to create the plans. Sales were going very well on the conversion project, and he had started the development he was planning when we met. We needed a certain amount of pre-sales to put the financing together. This development would have to be sold without the benefit of models. We created the plans, had them drawn up and created a miniature model of the development to display under glass. That was all I needed. By this time my energy was so high and my mind was so clear that things seemed to happen almost automatically. I continued to work with the principles of creation that I now understood and it was most interesting to see how well they worked in a business setting. Every evening I would take some time to get very clear in my mind what I wanted to happen the next day. I would visualize it, accept it, and it happened. I found people calling me or walking into my office whom I had visualized seeing or talking with the day before. My work became easier and easier. I expected that everyone I met would want to help me, and they did. People would buy a townhouse, then they would bring their friends to buy one. Someone even rang my doorbell one evening and said, "I would like to buy one of the townhouses you are selling."

It was a small development, only twenty-seven townhouses plus a pool and clubhouse. I sold all the units in a very short time. The developer wanted to know how I sold so many townhouses, and if I could teach others to sell the way I did.

It was obviously a different way of selling. It was quite clear to me to see why my sales were so easy and why others found it difficult. Just as with all of our experiences, we get what we expect. I knew that my vision was indeed coming about and would manifest within the year. My focus was on helping others fulfill their visions. I wanted everyone to be as happy with their townhouses as I was with mine. I helped them change the design slightly to better fit their needs. I also helped them with their financing, and showed them how to handle their money to make the most of what they had. I knew I was taken care of; consequently, I was not concerned with myself. I was only there to help them. This mind-set sent out an energy that attracted people to me. In observing some of the other sales people, I could see that they, too, were putting out an energy. Many times that energy was one of need to make a sale. The prospective customer felt the energy of someone trying to get something from them, so they protected themselves by leaving.

This is exactly how we create all of the problems in our lives. If we feel a need, we put out an energy that demands that belief be fulfilled. We can never create what we want when we feel needy. In order to create the life we want for ourselves, we must feel whole and complete within ourselves. Our creations are not external; they come from within us. In my original discovery I began to feel whole and complete. I knew I was not separate from anyone or anything else. Separateness is only in form. **Everything in existence is love expressing intelligently through energy**. This is a basic nonchanging law of nature or principle of life that we must understand in order to create the lives we desire.

Creating My Ideal Partner

Let all seen enjoyments lead to the unseen fountain from whence they flow.—T.C. Haliburton, nineteenth century Canadian historian

My experiment had worked. I had worked with the principles that I had discovered and created my vision just as I had envisioned it. It had been one year since beginning this adventure and I was now living in my new townhouse—with my new furniture including my grand piano—decorated just the way I wanted it. I was also driving my new bronze Cutlass Supreme Oldsmobile, and my second townhouse was rented as planned. I had experienced being on top of the world. My energy had been very high, my mind very clear, and my plans and desires had materialized with the greatest of ease.

The developer I was working with had started two more developments and I was now the new sales manager. I was excited to see if I could teach others to function the way I had been functioning. However, I was experiencing a little less energy and a little less clarity, so it was becoming a little more difficult to keep up my usual pace. Gradually I was moving back toward the level of functioning I had always experienced before my discovery.

I now had two full-time jobs. As a flight attendant, I could fly a trip to Hawaii, which left on Saturday morning and returned Sunday morning. I didn't work the return trip, so I was able to sleep on the flight. On Sundays my flight arrived about 7:00 A.M. I would come home from my trip, take a shower and hold an open house on Sunday afternoon. I was having so much success and so much fun that I had stopped doing my daily routine which had brought me to this new level of functioning. I knew it was time to let go of some of my activity and get back to my daily practice of the breathing exercises, stretching exercises, meditation and focusing techniques.

Circumstances seemed to take care of the situation. I had pre-sold more than enough townhouses and condominiums to secure financing for our latest project, but money had become very tight. In fact, none was available in our area due to a state law that wouldn't allow interest rates to go to the level that existed in other parts of the country. My real estate career was over for now. This turn of events gave me time to evaluate my life again.

I found myself asking again what my purpose was in being here and what should I be doing with my life. The answers came very clearly: I should fully understand these principles and share them with others. I didn't know how to share what I had discovered with others. When I asked about it, the answer that came was, "When the time is right, you will know." I knew it was now time to go back to my process and try to discover what had actually happened, why it happened, and how I could help others understand and work with these principles to create what they wanted in their lives.

It took several years, but I finally realized what had happened for me. The routine of things I had put together, and was practicing on a daily basis, had strengthened my nervous system so it was capable of a higher level of functioning. It was clear to me that this is our natural state, but a state I had never experienced before, nor did I know anyone else who had. What I had created through my routine was a process for releasing stress stored in the nervous system, and strengthening the system so it was capable of a more refined level of functioning. It was simply high-level wellness. I had previously believed that if I wasn't sick, and if I felt OK, I was healthy. Now it was very clear that there are much higher levels of health possible. And if it was possible for me, it had to also be possible for others.

I knew I had discovered something of great value, and that I must understand how it works in order to create a way to share it with others. I read lots of books to gain a greater understanding of stress and the nervous system and how they interact. We all experience stress in our lives. Dr. Hans Selye who devoted his life to the study of stress, said there are two kinds of stress: he called them eustress and distress. Eustress could be called good stress, the stress necessary to keep us functioning. Distress is created when the system has become overloaded.

Dr. Seyle defines stress as any demand made on the nervous system. The nervous system carries all the messages from the senses to the brain and dispatches all of the replies to all parts of the body. Using his definition, we can see how much stress we have in our lives. There are many kinds of stress. Emotional stress is what we usually think of when we think of stress, but there are also environmental stresses, and demands for our attention coming from many different directions constantly. When the nervous system becomes overloaded, it simply stores the demands until it has time to catch up. This is similar to the way an office worker would stack paperwork on his desk when he had more work than he could handle. As we can see, in time this would create problems.

This stored stress in the nervous system prevents the system from functioning at its full capacity. This is a process that takes place over time; it is such a gradual process that we never notice it. Most of us begin overstressing the nervous system while we are still children; therefore, we never know the full capacity of the nervous system as an adult. If the system was not overstressed, a good night's sleep would take care of revitalizing it, so it could function at its peak capacity. Since most of us have regularly overstressed the system all of our lives, it takes additional repair to bring it back to its natural state. As doctors will tell you, our bodies know how to heal and strengthen themselves. When we are sick, the first thing a doctor will tell us is to get plenty of rest. Given a sufficient amount of rest, the body releases stress and strengthens itself. Most of us have never been fully rested since becoming adults. There is so much stress in our lives that unless we make a conscious effort to reduce it, stress continues to mount. Gradually, we have a little less energy and our minds aren't quite as clear as we would like. But we never notice, because this is also happening to others, and we think it is natural, or at least inevitable—if we think about it at all.

The process of doing the breathing and stretching exercises, enjoying a healthy diet (which just happened), getting sufficient sleep, meditating and using focusing techniques, released the stress that had been stored in my nervous system and strengthened the system so it was capable of functioning much more effectively. This more refined functioning of the nervous system automatically connects the conscious awareness with intuitive knowingness. Intuition is a natural capacity of a strong nervous system.

Nothing in my background had prepared me for an experience like this; it just happened. I soon started wondering if others had also had such experiences. Again I went back to the study of psychology, and discovered Abraham Maslow's work published in the 1960s. Until Maslow's time, beginning in the 1950s, the field of psychology had been dominated by the study of psychologically sick people. Maslow was the first to study psychologically healthy people. Through his studies he discovered a few people who functioned quite differently than most of the population. He called these people self-actualized. They were functioning from a much higher level of health than most. Maslow found these people were highly intuitive and highly creative. In fact, in reading Maslow's studies of self-actualized people, I discovered he clearly described my experiences. I was not the only one who had these experiences, but I knew I had discovered a process for helping others release stress, strengthen the nervous system, and actually move into a new world from what most of us experience. I knew I must find a way to share this.

My friends knew something wonderful had happened for me and they wanted to understand it. They were asking how they could also experience this. I didn't know. I tried to explain it, but it didn't help much. I had to create a course that would give them the same experience. I told them things to do, but without a full understanding they were not able to follow through on their own. I knew that when the time was right I would know how to share this knowledge, but that didn't keep it from being quite frustrating while I waited and searched for the answer as to how to share my experience.

What I had intuitively known from the beginning was that I must experiment with this process in my own life until I fully understood how it worked. It was probably time to experience using the creative process again for myself. The first question was, "What do I want?" I was single and truly wanted someone to share my life with. My life had changed dramatically, and I longed for someone to share all aspects of it with me. I knew my life would be about these new discoveries and I wanted to share it with someone. I didn't know anyone who had any knowledge of this kind of thing. However, I did know that I could attract someone into my life who would be perfectly suited to me in every way. I simply needed to get clear on what that person would be like. I knew he existed, but I needed to know him in my mind in order to attract him into my life.

If he were perfectly suited for a relationship with me where we could share our work and life together, what would he be like? First, he would have some knowledge about the kind of things I am now working with, plus a very strong interest in this field. He should probably be a psychologist. It would also be good if he had some background in business. Of course, he would be intelligent and good looking. He would also be fun to be with. I can get pretty focused on work, so he should like fun things to help me stay light. He would also be curious—an explorer. He would enjoy handling some details, such as planning vacations. He would be very supportive and easy to live with. He would be thoughtful and considerate. We would love each other deeply, and he would appreciate me for being who I am. It would be a very special relationship and everyone we met would be inspired by it.

19

I worked with my vision until I got as clear as I could about my future partner. I tried to cover all the bases because I knew if I didn't get clear, whatever I believed, on a deep level, would indeed show up. Once I felt I was as clear as possible, I created visions of the two of us being together, working, exploring and having fun.

Next I had to check my deep beliefs. My girlfriends and I had a number of them that immediately came to my attention. Some of the things we usually said were, "There just aren't any good men around," or, "Why can't I meet someone really special?" This, of course, assumed that anyone I would want to be with didn't exist or at least wasn't going to be in my life. Time to reprogram that kind of thinking: I now knew that these negative ideas didn't need to be true for us. They were simply something that we had accepted and were creating in our lives. Even though I knew better, my beliefs still needed a little work. I worked with it until I could fully accept this ideal person in my life and fully expected him to appear at any minute.

It took a little time, but guess what? He showed up. I was at a spiritual retreat for a weekend, and when I came down the stairs to the dining room for dinner, I noticed a very good-looking man observing me. Most of the people at the retreat were younger than I, but he was obviously older and looked most interesting. It was a buffet serving, and when I got in line I noticed that he was right behind me. We started talking in line and then sat together for dinner. He told me that he was a psychologist, but was now in the business world. He had grown up in a family business, just as I had. After a few years in business with his father and brother he decided to go back to school, where he received doctorates in both theology and psychology. When his father retired he left the family business to him and his brother. The family business, however, did not motivate him, and he was at a crossroads in his life. I told him a little about myself and he seemed interested. We walked to class together and sat together. When the class was over I went back to my room, but I couldn't stop thinking about him. I thought of all the reasons why he probably wasn't the one. He was ten years older than I, and I had never dated anyone that much older before. The age difference was too much, and there were probably other reasons, but I did want to get to know him better. I finally went to sleep, but woke up a couple of times with the same thought: He is the one. I couldn't wait to get to class the next day. He was there, saving a seat for me. He asked me out for dinner on the Sunday night after the course was over. I invited him to follow me back to my townhouse after classes on Sunday afternoon, since I had placed some real estate ads in the paper, and needed to answer the calls before going out to dinner. He thoroughly investigated my townhouse while I made my calls. Yes, he was definitely an explorer.

We have now been married for twenty-one years, and have spent very little time apart since that snowy Sunday in Minnesota in 1977. I shared with him my discovery and he was most interested. I found that he had a lot of intellectual knowledge about these things, but his understanding was strictly on an intellectual level, even though he had seen what appeared to be miracles take place in his work. He knew that knowing something on the intellectual level is quite different from experiencing it in one's own life.

I knew the process I had gone through required a dedicated focus over time. He would be the perfect experiment, and he wanted to try it. I taught him the breathing exercises, stretching exercises and focusing techniques. He had already started to meditate on a regular basis. We practiced our routine together and he began to have some of the same experiences.

This was a time of change for him. Dean was phasing out of the family business and didn't know what he wanted to do. I told him he could create whatever he wanted, and he was ready to try it. He had a huge résumé and was serving on the board of directors for several companies. He had started to put out some feelers about possibilities, and was trying to go in a dozen different directions at the same time. I explained the need for one pointed focus, the creative process, and that we need not concern ourselves with what appeared to be available. I knew anything was possible. What he needed to do was get clear on what he wanted. After going through a lot of soul searching, reading *What Color Is Your Parachute?* and doing some exercises for getting clear, he finally said to me, "What I would really like is to have enough money at my disposal to research how the physical, mental and spiritual aspects of life interrelate." Along with that description he also informed me that this kind of opportunity didn't exist. I assured him that it would, once we created it. Dean continued to work on the vision, getting clear about where his office would be, the surroundings, how much he would be paid, etc. I helped him work with his vision, challenging his beliefs, until we had both accepted it and expected it to happen. And it did.

A couple of months later he was scheduled to speak at a conference in Houston, Texas, to a large audience of business executives from around the country. His subject was creativity in business. I joined him for the trip and we talked about the real possibilities for creativity in business. By now we both fully understood that we are all connected to all intelligence, and that it was possible for all of us to tap into that intelligence and know intuitively whatever we need to know. We were not at all sure the business world was ready for this, but he decided that he would tell them anyway.

We had a great trip, and the audience was very receptive. A few days after we had returned to Minneapolis, he got a phone call from the director of research and development for a large company based in Tacoma, Washington. He said that he and others from their company had been in the audience in Texas and had heard terms that they had not heard before. They wanted to know more about the term "creative intelligence." They asked if Dean could meet them at the airport in Minneapolis to discuss it further. He agreed, and asked me to join them for this meeting. We met in the Top Flight Club for about two and a half hours. They had another flight out, and left with an invitation for us to meet with them in their offices in Tacoma in a couple of weeks.

The company had beautiful offices in Tacoma, and we were very much impressed with their research and development department. They were well aware of the changes that were taking place in the world today, and were preparing for the paradigm shift. They were aware of the benefit of meditation and had plans for meditation rooms for their employees. We discussed intuition and how it could work in business. They asked Dean if he knew any CEOs who were using intuition to make their business decisions. He replied that he did. They concluded that this was a spiritual phenomenon, and thought that they should assemble what they were calling a spiritual advisory board, made up of highly intuitive people, to advise them and possibly other businesses.

I offered my understanding that intuition is not a way of gathering abstract information. My experience was that what comes to us intuitively is related to what we truly want to know. I was not able to intuitively know anything that was not related to what I personally needed to know. I explained that we are all intuitive and can develop these abilities, and my suggestion was to develop the intuitive abilities of the people involved in the business. The meeting concluded with their request that we decide what needed to be done.

Dean was ready to start putting together a board of highly intuitive people. I knew that wouldn't work; I knew that we must somehow put together a program to help people develop their own intuitive abilities. We were discussing what to do on the flight home, when Dean picked up a copy of *Corporate Report* magazine that happened to be in the seat pocket. The cover story was about Lynn Charlson, a highly intuitive Minneapolis man who had used his intuitive abilities to create a very successful business. The article explained that he had a number of patents on farm equipment. It also said he was considered to be the father of fluid hydraulics. Dean was determined to meet Charlson, and called shortly after we returned home. He was well protected from the public, however, and it took about a month of calling until one day Dean called and Lynn Charlson answered the phone. Dean introduced himself and explained that he had read the article in *Corporate Report* and would like to meet with him. They set a time.

Lynn Charlson, the inventor, was the founder and president of the Char-Lynn company. He and Dean had a great time at their meeting, discussing each other's background and their common interests. Charlson told him that he grew up on a farm in North Dakota, came to Minneapolis while still in his teens, and worked as a night clerk at a local hotel. It seems that a number of engineers stayed at the hotel and he listened to them talking about their problems and needs. He said he realized that he could intuitively sense how to solve their problems, and to the amazement of the engineers, his suggestions worked. After he became quite proficient with this, he got together enough money to start his own engineering company. He hired some well-educated engineers to work for him, but he would go out to the farms and talk to the farmers about their needs himself. Then he would come back and, he said, he would meditate on their needs. A solution would then appear to him in his mind's eye in three dimensions. He would take it to his engineers and they would say it couldn't be done. However, he knew it could, because he had seen it in his mind. He said many times he would have to build a prototype himself because his engineers couldn't believe it until he showed it to them. This was how all his patents had come about.

Dean was very much intrigued, and loved talking with him. They were both very curious about how these things happen. A couple of weeks later he called Dean and asked him to come over to his office for a visit. In this meeting he explained that he had sold his company, and now he wanted to create a foundation to do research in the physical sciences, mental sciences and the spiritual aspect of life and how they interrelate. He asked Dean if he would like to help him do this and be the director of his research foundation. This was it—exactly what Dean had envisioned and had been focusing his attention on creating.

Lynn Charlson had become very wealthy as a result of all of his patents, and he now wanted to put much of this money into a research foundation to do exactly what Dean wanted to do. They agreed to work together and the details unfolded exactly as Dean had envisioned them.

Dean worked with the foundation for seven years, and they spent millions of dollars doing some very fine research and working with a number of universities and other organizations. Even though they did some very valuable work, Charlson's desire was not fulfilled. He wanted to be able to teach others how to tap into their intuitive abilities as he did, combining that with their intellectual education, thereby creating far greater creativity for the students and the world. They conducted many good workshops, but even though people learned new concepts, nothing much seemed to change in their lives. Charlson was very fortunate in that he simply had this capability, but he didn't know how to develop it in others.

I, on the other hand, had not been fortunate enough to be born with this intuitive ability, but I had discovered how to develop it within myself, and had also been able to now share it with Dean.

Creating a Process for Sharing

Man's capacities have never been measured, nor are we to judge what he can do by any precedents, so little has been tried.—Henry David Thoreau

I was serving on the board of directors for an organization that I really hoped would succeed. The president of the organization was having problems communicating with the board. There were a number of different views on the purpose and direction it was to take and much controversy as to who should be the leader. I knew that if everyone could see the situation more clearly, things could be worked out to the satisfaction of all, or we could at least devise a plan that would work for the greatest good of the organization.

For many years I had known that I must put together a program for sharing my discovery, and now was the perfect opportunity to put something together and test it. I believed I could set up a program to teach the board members the process I had used to get to a level of much greater clarity, and we could then save this organization.

It took a couple of months to design the course. By the time it was completed several board members had resigned, but the remaining members agreed to do the course. I knew it was a process over time, and I didn't know how much time was needed. I knew it was about total commitment and choosing to devote the time necessary to learn and integrate into their lives

27

a whole new way of living. There had to be a definite commitment and enough time to create new habits.

The Charlson Research Foundation was doing research on the significance of numbers, and the number seven seemed to mean fullness and completion. Since I didn't know how many sessions it would take, seven seemed like a good number. It also seemed that we should have seven participants for this pilot study. Since there were not seven board members left, I decided to invite a few other friends to join us in this experiment. I told all of the prospective participants that I knew it was possible for all of us to increase our energy, think more clearly, and create anything we wanted. They were all excited to try the program. I told them it would require at least an hour every day to do the stretching exercises, breathing exercises, meditation, focusing techniques and working with our choices. They all made a commitment to show up every other week for a three-and-one-half-hour class for seven sessions and do the assignments every day.

Since schedules had to be changed several times, the course lasted almost six months, but we did have great results. The participants each got very clear about what they wanted to create in their lives. The question they each asked themselves was the same one that I had asked Dean: "If you knew you could create anything you wanted, what would you create?" We worked through different techniques to help them get as clear as possible on what they wanted to create. I asked them to each come up with seven things they wanted to create in their lives within the next three months. I told them to forget about how they were going to create it, just get clear about what they would want if there was nothing that could keep them from creating it.

It was fun watching them break free from fears and old beliefs, and even more fun watching them create their dreams and desires. The class was made up of a variety of personalities, occupations and desires. In terms of occupations, there was a stockbroker, a bank vice president, a manufacturer's representative, a flight attendant, an administrative assistant, a salesman and a real estate broker. The stockbroker focused on making more money, and his commissions soared. The bank vice president was the president of the organization we were working with. His vision for the organization became very clear, and he was able to reorganize and move forward on a successful path.

By the end of the course each person was experiencing life on a different level. They had all created the seven things they wanted to create, or at least were able to see that they had made great strides in moving toward them. They were so excited about their experiences that they wanted to share them with some of their friends, and asked me to do another class. That was in 1984, and that was the beginning of Unlimited Futures. Since that time, thousands of people have participated in the course with wonderful results.

In the meantime, Dean and I were creating our dream house.

I knew my purpose in life was to share my discovery with others, and now I had created a program that would allow me to do that. We knew we would need a place to hold the courses, so with the understanding of the importance of environment we created a home with offices and classrooms, a pool, a tennis court, and walking paths within a forest of beautiful trees on a lake. It was our dream house, and also a place we wanted to share with others. It was spectacular—exactly what we had envisioned. We knew we wanted to work together, so in the summer of 1985 Dean left the research foundation and came to work with me at Unlimited Futures.

The company grew and more and more people discovered their own ability to take charge of their lives and create the life they wanted for themselves. I also created an executive development program and we were able to share that program with groups of people in many of the major corporations within the Twin Cities.

We realized that we had something of great value to people, and wanted to share it with more and more people. The question was how. Again I learned that life, for each of us, is about our own personal growth. Just as in the beginning when I first discovered these techniques for personal growth, it took much longer than I had hoped to discover how to share them. I grew through all of my trials and errors. Now we were looking at ways of expanding our programs. We tried training other people to facilitate the classes, and that worked for a while, but we decided that if we were going to share the program with many people we needed centers or facilities in other locations. We tried training facilitators to start their own centers, which didn't work.

Our vision then turned to putting the course on video tape. Although there is an advantage to taking the program in a group because of the bonding that occurs when people share an important experience together, we decided that the video tape should make up for that in convenience. This way people could purchase the course on video and experience it in the privacy of their own homes or wherever they chose. The course could be taken with friends and loved ones or alone. The most valuable part is that it can be done over and over until it has become totally integrated into one's life. This is not a three-month course, it is a lifetime experience. This course is about understanding some basic laws of nature or principles of life and living in harmony with them. It is about taking charge of our lives and creating them the way we want them to be. It is a lifetime process for all of us. Each accomplishment brings us to the next challenge, but it is most gratifying to know that we can meet that challenge, and that it soon will be another accomplishment.

This discovery has seemed the most natural and fulfilling experience of my life. It has not been just one experience, but an ongoing experience that has allowed me to take charge of my life and create the life that I continually choose for myself.

We now know that each of us has the potential to create whatever we choose. Whether we want to create inner peace and joy for ourselves, happy fulfilling relationships, a successful career that is fulfilling and rewarding, wealth, or the perfect mate for ourselves, the principles work the same way in each case. We simply have to know the principles and prepare ourselves to be capable of working with them to create whatever we want.

Part Two

A New Paradigm/A New World

What is Self-Actualization?

*The goal of education . . . is ultimately the self-
actualization of a person, the becoming fully human, the
development of the fullest height that the human species
can stand up to. . . .*—Abraham Maslow,
twentieth century American psychologist

Abraham Maslow speaks of a self-actualized person as one who
is psychologically healthy or mature. Here is a list of some of
the characteristics that Maslow found in the self-actualized
people he studied.

1. They are healthy—physically, mentally, emotionally and
   spiritually.

2. They are superior in their perception of reality, which even-
   tuates in a superior ability to reason and perceive truth.
   The consequence is that they live more in the real world
   of nature rather than in the man-made mass of concepts,
   abstractions, expectations, beliefs and stereotypes that
   most people confuse with the real world.

3. They are more accepting of self, others and nature. They
   find it possible to accept themselves and their own nature
   without chagrin or complaint or, for that matter, even without thinking about the matter very much. They see human nature as it is and not as they would prefer it to be.

4. They exhibit spontaneity, simplicity and naturalness. One
   consequence or correlation of this characteristic is that

they have codes of ethics that are relatively autonomous and individual rather than conventional.

5. They are problem-centered rather than ego-centered. They customarily have some mission in life, some task to fulfill, some problem outside themselves, which enlists much of their energies.

6. They have a quality of detachment and a need for privacy. They can be solitary without harm to themselves and without discomfort. Furthermore, it is true for almost all that they positively like solitude and privacy to a definitely greater degree than the average person. It is possible for them to remain above the battle, to remain unruffled, undisturbed by that which produces turmoil in others. They find it easy to be aloof, reserved, and also calm and serene; thus it becomes possible for them to take personal misfortunes without reacting as the ordinary person does.

7. They are quite autonomous, independent of culture and environment. They are in charge of their own lives, active agents of their own will.

8. Self-actualized people have continued freshness of appreciation. They have the wonderful capability to appreciate again and again, freshly and naively, the basic goods of life, with awe, pleasure, wonder and even ecstasy, however stale these experiences may have become to others.

9. They are highly intuitive and many of them have peak experiences, which allow them to see the entire universe in its fullness as an integrated and unified whole.

10. They are compassionate.

11. In interpersonal relations they are capable of more fusion, greater love, more perfect identification, more obliteration of the ego boundaries, than other people would consider possible.

12. They are democratic characters. They can be and are friendly with anyone of suitable character regardless of class, education, political belief, race or color. It often seems as if they are not even aware of these differences.

13. They have unusual powers of discrimination. These individuals are strongly ethical; they have definite moral standards; they do right and do not do wrong. Needless to

say, their notions of right and wrong and of good and evil are often not the conventional ones.

14. They have an unhostile sense of humor. They do not consider funny what the average man considers to be funny. Thus, they do not laugh at hostile humor.

15. They are highly creative. Each one shows in one way or another a special kind of creativeness or originality or inventiveness that has certain peculiar characteristics.

16. Resistance to enculturation—they get along with the culture in various ways, but all of them, in a certain profound and meaningful sense, resist enculturation and maintain a certain inner detachment from the culture in which they are immersed.

17. They do not have a fear of the unknown. In fact they embrace it. It simply becomes something to explore.

18. They are more objective (in every sense) than average people. This is true even when the problem concerns themselves, their own wishes, motives, hopes, or aspirations.

19. They have the ability to concentrate to a degree not usual in the ordinary person.

20. They are autonomous, make their own decisions, are self-governing, and are active, responsible, self-disciplined, deciding agents rather than pawns, or helplessly "determined" by others. They make up their own minds, come to their own decisions, are self-starters, and are responsible for themselves and their own destinies.

21. The self-actualized person no longer strives in the ordinary sense. The motivation of ordinary men is a striving for the basic need gratifications that they lack. But self-actualized people, in fact, lack none of these gratifications; they work, and are ambitious, even though in an unusual sense. For them, motivation is just character growth.

22. The self-actualized count on blessings. They retain a constant sense of good fortune and gratitude for it.

If you would like to know more about Maslow's findings from his study of self-actualized people I would highly recommend reading his book, *Motivation and Personality*.

This chart depicts human needs from the most basic to the most refined. The ordinary person spends his/her time and

Maslow's Hierarchy of Needs

energy in the pursuit of the fulfillment of these needs. On the first level we find the most urgent needs, which include food, shelter, clothing, etc. Then the next level relates to one's need for love and belonging. Everyone needs to feel appreciated, cared for, and a part of a family or group of people. The next level is about one's need for respect and self-esteem—the need to feel good about one's self. Then comes the need for autonomy. Everyone wants to be in charge of his own life. We all want to feel capable and in control—self-governing.

The difference between the motivation of the self-actualized person and others lies in their perception of how life works. The self-actualized person understands that there are laws of nature or principles of life that are responsible for what happens in the material world of experience. They know that if they live in harmony with these principles their needs and desires will be fulfilled. Other people do not have access to this knowledge and, therefore, have different beliefs about how to fulfill their needs. This lack of understanding creates stress, struggle and an unfulfilled life.

Self-actualized people come in all different sizes, shapes and colors and their personalities are as varied as the rest of society. The things that distinguish them from others are rarely seen. Self-actualization is about an inner state of being. The self-actualized person has access to a different way of knowing.

"Know thyself" is advice that has been handed down by the wise throughout time. The self-actualized person knows himself in a way that has not been discovered by the majority of society. The self-actualized person has discovered another dimension of self. This could be considered the spiritual dimension of one's self. It has nothing to do with religion; it is the experience of knowing one's self on a totally different level than is available to the five senses and the intellect.

People living in what I call a three-dimensional world have only the five senses and the intellect to use as tools of perception. In this state we can never see the big picture because the senses and the intellect are limited. The intellect is only capable of seeing parts.

This reminds me of a story I once heard about a group of men who were looking at an elephant through holes in a wooden fence. One man, who saw only the elephant's leg, said the elephant was like a tree. Another, seeing only the elephant's body, described the elephant as a gray wall. One who saw only the elephant's tusk, thought the elephant was a marble pillar. Yet another, seeing only the elephant's tail, described an elephant as a curly snake. None of them could know what the elephant looked like, since they could only see part of him.

The same thing is true for us when we have only the senses and the intellect for perceiving the nature of life. This is why we make poor choices, and create all of the unpleasantness of our lives. It is like trying to put together a puzzle with most of the pieces missing.

The self-actualized person has access to the wholeness of life. He has developed another tool to use for perception, which we call intuition. Intuitive awareness comes from the level of wholeness. From this level we can see not only all the parts, but also how all the parts fit together. Consequently, the self-actualized person sees life from a totally different perspective and has the ability to function in a much more effective manner.

The self-actualized person perceives the nature of life. He sees the perfection in all of creation, and becomes aware of the laws of nature that govern the material world, and our life experiences. When one becomes aware of these principles, it becomes clear how to work with them to create the life one wants.

Self-actualization is a human potential. It is something we can all grow into and experience for ourselves. In order to do this we must take some time to prioritize our lives. Our first choice must be to focus our attention on the creation of optimal health. Part Four of this book provides step-by-step guidelines for creating optimal health, which includes the growth and development of self-actualization. This state of being prepares people to take charge of their lives and create whatever they choose.

Laws of Nature that **5** Govern Our Lives

All that a man has externally in multicapacity is
intrinsically One. Here all the blades of grass, wood and
stone, all things are One. This is the deepest depth and
thereby am I completely captivated.—Meister Eckhart,
thirteenth century German philosopher

Laws of nature are unchanging principles that determine our experiences. They are the principles that govern how life works. Gravity is a law of nature that governs how objects relate to the earth. Laws of nature are unseen, but are always affecting outcomes. In order to understand how life works, we need to understand at least some of these laws.

Here are seven laws of nature that will help us understand the role we each play in creating our own experiences.

The first law is: **Everything in existence is Love expressing intelligently through Energy**. I use the word Love to identify the source of creation. Whether we look at it from a scientific perspective or a theological perspective, the result is the same. Where I use the term Love, the theologian would use the word God; the physicist would use the term unified field.

The source has been referred to by numerous names in sacred writings from around the world. Most of us are familiar with the name God. There are a number of synonyms for God, some of which are Love, Light, Principle, Intelligence, Mind or Spirit. I have chosen the word Love because this book is about learning how to experience our source, and I believe our experience of Love, and the power of Love, best brings us to this experience.

Einstein's unified field theory, in layman's terms, states that everything in existence originates from and returns to the same source. Therefore, everything is an expression of this source which I am calling Love. All intelligence is also contained in this source. The Source (Love) creates all of creation as an expression of itself. Imagine in your mind a large circle with a dot in the center. Let the circumference of the circle represent all of creation, and let the dot in the center represent the source. In order to express itself the source moves in an intelligent way which creates energy. Einstein's theory of relativity tells us that everything in existence is energy.

Energy can be either gross or refined. A rock is gross or dense energy, the human body is a more refined energy, and the energy that makes up the human mind is more refined than the energy of the body. What appears to be matter is just energy vibrating at a very rapid rate. Scientists tell us that what appears to be solid or matter is actually empty space.

All energy is intelligent and invincible. Energy is never destroyed, it only changes form. If we can understand this, we can then begin to understand how creation is created, and our role in it.

When asked "Who are you?" most people would say that they are a doctor, attorney, executive, secretary or a mother, wife, husband, or father, or maybe they would identify themselves by their religion or philosophy. This, however, is not who we *are*. These are ways in which we relate to other people and the world around us. When you take away all of these kinds of identification, then who are you?

My hope here is that you can see that you cannot exist as a separate entity. We are each whole and complete within ourselves, but we exist in relationship to others. On the spiritual level we are Love (the source), on the mental level we are Intelligence. We are all connected to Universal Intelligence, and on the physical level we are all Energy. We are all made of the same material, and everything in existence is connected. We and other expressions in the universe are only separate in form.

The next question then is: "How do forms come into being?" This leads us to the second law of nature we want to explore, which is: **Thought directs energy.** From ancient science we find that Heraclitus (535–475 B.C.) states, "The universe is generated not according to time, but according to thought." In modern science we find Sir James Jeans (1877–1946) states, "The universe begins to look more like a great thought than a great machine." Sir Arthur Eddington, a British physicist, puts it this way: "The stuff of the world is mind stuff."

Thought creates movement; therefore, we could say that when Love (the Source) thinks—creation occurs. It is the thought, intent or belief of the thinker that directs energy or attracts the energy necessary to manifest that thought or belief. As expressions of the Source (Love), we also create our world of experiences in the same way. We could say that spiritual energy directs mental energy, which in turn directs physical energy. Consequently, what we experience is a result of our thoughts.

The next law of nature that comes into play here is **the law of attraction and repulsion.** Our attention, thoughts and deepest beliefs work together to create forms. The law of attraction and repulsion acts like a vacuum to pull in the energy necessary to fill these forms. Energy is always readily available for creating anything, but what we experience will be whatever we truly believe in and are focusing our attention on. The law of attraction and repulsion works both ways. This law repels the energy that does not fit the form created by our thoughts, beliefs and attention.

You have heard the statement, "What comes from us returns to us, or what goes around comes around." This is due to the law of attraction and repulsion. It works like a boomerang. The energy that we create through our thoughts goes out into the energy fields and attracts to itself its perfect reflection, and returns it to us. Anything is possible, but only what we believe in will be our experience.

This brings us to the next law we want to explore, which is **Giving and Receiving are two sides of the same coin.** You can't have one without the other. If someone wants to give you a gift, but you say, "I can't take that from you," nothing happens, right?

Most of us think that we would certainly accept whatever we want if it were given to us, but the truth is that most of us do not know how to receive. Since we now know that everything is energy and readily available for forming into whatever we want, we can see that anything and everything is being offered to us. Why aren't we accepting it? Because we have not understood the nature of energy, and how it works.

Another law of nature, which fits in here, is that **Everything in the relative world is always changing.** Energy, which is the building block of everything, is always moving. Energy freely moves from one form to another. Energy flows in and out of everything and builds whatever form is appropriate. For example, Dr. Deepak Chopra tells us that the body is always renewing itself. In a recent lecture I attended, he said that the body we came into his lecture with was not the body that was there at the time, because energy is always flowing in and out of the body and recreating all the cells of the body.

The energy of the universe flows in and out, in the same manner in which we breathe. We breathe the energy into our bodies in a form that regenerates our cells, which is receiving. Then we breathe the energy out in a form which regenerates the plants in our environment; thus, we are giving it back. The plants do the same thing. They breathe out energy in the form that we need to regenerate our bodies. The flow must continue in order to create healthy bodies for both animals and plants. If we try to hold on to the air, it doesn't work. The same is true with everything; we must receive and must give in order to keep the flow of energy working in our lives. We will discuss this further, and look at how this works in other areas of our lives.

The next law of nature is that **Beliefs are simply information that we have accepted as truth.** We become very attached to our beliefs because we think they are true.

42

We have experienced the truth of them. What actually happens, however, is that our thoughts and beliefs create our experiences, which in turn validate our beliefs. In fact most of our beliefs have been handed down to us from our parents, friends and our culture and in most cases we have never questioned them. As children we learn how to manage in the world by observing our parents and the people around us. We are told the beliefs of the people in our lives over and over, so naturally we accept them as truth. Unless we stop and question these beliefs, they keep running our lives, and we keep creating the things that our family and culture believes in, because we have accepted them as truth.

When we begin to investigate, we soon see that what we believed to be true at one time turns out not to be true. For many years people believed the earth was flat, and that was their experience. We see the same phenomenon in reports from scientists in the medical arena. Something that is believed to be of great benefit to our health turns out to actually be damaging. What we have accepted as truth is also in the relative world, which is always changing. The only absolute (nonchanging) truths we can know are the laws of nature.

Our beliefs form the energy that creates our experiences, but we are free to believe whatever we choose. This brings us to the seventh law of nature, which is **We all make our own choices**.

Other people may coerce us, threaten us, or present us with numerous ideas for our consideration, but ultimately we must choose. Even when we choose not to choose, we have still made a choice. This choice is to give someone else the power to make our decisions for us, but that is still a choice. We ourselves give the power to other people and situations that control our lives.

This is a principle that many of us are not aware of, but when we look into it, we realize that it is a fact of life. In our lives we experience the results of the choices we have made. We may not realize we have options, but that again is a belief which we can change. We always have options, even though we may not be able to see them at any given time.

Once we accept the fact that we are indeed making our own choices, we are able to take our own power back, if we have given it away to beliefs that do not serve us well. Many times we hear the statement "I *have* to_____ (fill in the blank)."

When we catch ourselves making such a statement, it is very helpful to change that statement to "I am *choosing* to." This makes us aware of the fact that we have options, and we are indeed in charge of our choices, and will experience the consequences of them.

We will look at examples of how these principles of life are working in our experiences as we continue on.

Why Are We Not Self-Actualized?

*Consciousness is a source of self-cognition quite apart
from and independent of reason. Through his reason man
observes himself, but only through consciousness does he
know himself.*—Leo Tolstoy

Self-actualization is our natural state. Why, then, are we not all
self-actualized? What blocks this natural ability from our awareness?

Let's start by looking at consciousness. There are many
states of consciousness, but here we need only look at and understand the three major states of consciousness. First is con-
scious-awareness, the state you are in right now, as you read this
book. We could describe the conscious mind as present awareness. On this level we find thinking, discrimination, choice, reason and logic. The second level of consciousness is what we call
the subconscious. This is the part of our consciousness that
simply stores information. The subconscious cannot discrimi-
nate or choose, it simply stores data. All the information that is
taken in through the senses is stored in the subconscious. Much
information goes into the subconscious that we are not consciously aware of. The information stored in the subconscious
is used to create our beliefs. These beliefs create our experiences.

Many of our beliefs are not on the conscious level and we
have never made a conscious choice about them. We will dis-

cuss this in more detail when we look at beliefs. The third level of consciousness that we want to look at here is what we call the superconscious. The superconscious is all intelligence, all knowledge. It is a part of who we are. We access the superconscious on the level of silence, and knowledge from this level is what we call intuitive awareness.

If this is a part of who we are, then why are we not aware of it? Remember the first law of nature we discussed: "Everything in existence is Love expressing intelligently through Energy." The superconscious is what we could call universal intelligence. The reason we are unable to access it is due to the energy aspect of who we are. Earlier we talked about the fact that energy expresses itself in different levels of density or refinement. We talked about a rock being a very dense form of energy and the body and mind being a more refined energy. The superconscious or universal intelligence is the most highly refined form of energy. In order for us to access the superconscious our mind/body energy must become more highly refined.

Energy

If we are observant, we can see and feel the energy movement in our lives. Notice the feeling of heaviness when someone around you is being very negative, maybe making statements about how bad things are, and predicting that they are going to get worse. The energy within everything in the environment becomes more dense. Then also notice how you feel when you are in the presence of someone who is very upbeat and positive. There is a feeling of lightness. The energy is becoming more refined. Better yet, notice the energy within yourself when you are thinking negative and positive thoughts. You will be able to feel the difference. Another good test is to observe the energy in your body when you get into an argument or encounter some form of conflict. You can feel the energy in your body contracting, becoming strained and uncomfortable. You can see how this kind of energy or stress can create disease and/or malfunction in the body. Most doctors agree that at least ninety-eight percent of all illness is stress-related. Now let's look at how stress affects our ability to become self-actualized.

Stress

Hans Selye, who dedicated his life to the study of stress, defines stress as any demand made on the body. He says there are two kinds of stress, which he calls eustress and distress. Eustress is created by the positive, exciting experiences in our lives, and distress is created by the negative things. If stress is any demand made on the body, we can see that both positive and negative experiences create demands on the mind/body system. The nervous system is responsible for carrying messages from the senses to the brain and dispatching the brain's response to all parts of the body.

A certain amount of stress is essential to life. The problems arise when there are more demands made on the mind/body system than it can handle. It is all work for the nervous system. Most of the time we are not even aware that we are overstressed, because the nervous system is also responsible for our perception. We usually think we are fine until something inappropriate occurs, like bursting into tears or yelling at someone. Uncontrollable laughter is also a sign that the nervous system is overstressed. When the system becomes overloaded it begins to malfunction. Have you noticed when you are overstressed that you are also unable to see possibilities? When we are overstressed we simply cannot see solutions to our problems. If the stress is not too severe, after we get a good night's sleep things look different. The rest has given the nervous system an opportunity to heal itself and return to its normal functioning.

Unfortunately, an overstressed nervous system is the reality most of us have created for ourselves. We usually start overstressing the nervous system even when we are children, and the stress mounts daily for most people. As the system becomes more and more stressed, the mind/body energy becomes less refined, and more dense. This is why we are not all self-actualized. The stress that builds up in our nervous systems over the years is what blocks our ability to connect with the superconscious on a conscious level. As we stated before, the superconscious is the most refined energy possible, and the mind/body energy must become more refined in order to be capable of experiencing it.

47

If we choose to become self-actualized, we must create a lifestyle that reduces stress and strengthens the nervous system on a daily basis. In Part Four of this book I have laid out a routine that, if practiced daily, will release the stress that has built up in the nervous system and will strengthen the system. This process, when practiced over time, will refine the energy of the mind/body system, thereby making the system capable of merging with the superconscious.

When the energy of the mind/body system is sufficiently refined, it automatically merges with the superconscious and we begin to know and understand the laws of nature and how life really works. This experience is like moving into a new world, a world of joy, bliss and understanding—a world where we intuitively know whatever we need to know to create the life we want. This is life on a completely different dimension from what we experience when we live in the world of the conscious and subconscious mind alone.

There is also another major factor that blocks our path to self-actualization. Let's take a look at it.

Beliefs

We are born into this world totally dependent upon other people to care for us and teach us how to survive and manage. At this time we have no conscious awareness of how anything works. We learn from others, and what they teach us is their beliefs. We are so busy trying to learn how to fulfill our needs that we seldom stop to question the information that we are given. They give us the best information they have, but they, too, came here trying to learn the same way we are. Consequently, the same information gets handed down from generation to generation. It is not until we stop and question the validity of this information that we discover that it might not be all that accurate, and there just might be a better way.

I heard a story once about a woman who always cut the end off her roast before cooking it. One day her daughter asked her why she did so each time. She explained that it was just how you cook a roast. She had always done it that way. Her mother had taught her how to cook, and that was what she was taught.

She had never thought about it before, but it did make her a bit curious, so she called her mother and asked her the same question. He mother replied that she had to cut the end off of her roast because her pan wasn't big enough to hold the entire roast. This is just an example of how something that worked at one time could be totally inappropriate for another, yet we keep carrying it forward.

Most of us believe many things that do not help us in creating what we want in our lives. We, of course, believe that our beliefs are correct, because they are our experiences. Since most of our beliefs have been programed into our subconscious without our even being aware of them, we haven't questioned them at all. But now that we know that these beliefs are creating our experiences, it may be time to start questioning.

There is always a dialogue going on in our minds. For people who are not self-actualized, this dialogue is between the conscious and the subconscious mind. When we think about something consciously, the subconscious begins to tell the conscious mind about all the information it has on the subject. Since it is the job of the subconscious to simply record and store all the information it comes into contact with, it has much conflicting information. Then the conscious mind tries to sort out all of this information to come up with what it thinks is a reasonable conclusion. What we do not realize is that all the information on which we have to make our decisions is whatever is stored in the subconscious. Since we have received all of this information from other people, we think that is the only way to get information. No one ever tells us that we are connected to universal intelligence, and can access all knowledge right within ourselves. The reason for this, of course, is because very few people know it. Very few people know it because of the incorrect beliefs we hold on to, and the stress that makes it impossible for the conscious mind to communicate with the superconscious.

We all have different beliefs which create our own experiences. Then there are cultural beliefs which most of us buy into. Since our information comes from other people, we believe that if a large number of people believe something, it must be true. Again we accept it without question.

Let's go back and take another look at a couple of the laws of nature that are governing our lives. Law # 5 is **"Everything in the relative world is always changing,"** and Law # 6 is **"Beliefs are simply information that we have accepted as truth."** Since everything is always changing, most of what we believe is probably obsolete. Then when we realize that beliefs are just information that we have accepted as truth, we can see that relative truth is also changeable. Law # 7 is **"We all make our own choices."** In light of this, we can see that many of the things we believe are not of benefit to us, and that we can, in fact, change them.

Every belief is simply someone's opinion. Your opinion is just as good as anyone else's. Once we understand what buying into other people's beliefs has created for us, we can begin to make some different choices. If we want to become self-actualized, and create unlimited futures for ourselves, we will need to change many of our beliefs. Many people do not believe that anyone can function from this more advanced level, and certainly not them. This, of course, needs to be changed. In Part Four we will discuss how we become aware of our beliefs and how to change them. Next let's look at how we actually create our experiences.

How We Create Our Own Experiences

There is an inmost center in us all, where truth abides in fullness.—Robert Browning, nineteenth century poet

Let's go back to our example of how creation is created. Remember, we used an example of a circle with a dot in the center. The dot represented the source of creation, and the larger circle represented what is created. When the source thinks (moves), energy is created. Everything is made of this energy.

My husband has a doctorate in theology, and he has discovered that these principles have all been written about in most sacred writings throughout history. However, for the most part we have completely missed them. He frequently uses a quote from the Bible to help explain this principle. The Bible says that we are all created in the image and likeness of God. Just as God, or whatever you call the source, created all of creation, we, in the same manner, create our own personal worlds.

Think of yourself as the dot in the center of your world. When you think, energy is created. That energy is subject to the law of attraction and repulsion. This energy goes out into the energy fields and attracts to itself whatever energy is appropriate to manifest that thought.

This is the basic principle, but it isn't quite that simple.

The conscious mind and the subconscious both play a role in our creations. A thought is a conscious act, but it is formed in the subconscious. Remember, the subconscious has stored all of the information it has ever received. Since the subconscious cannot make judgments, its only way of knowing what is important, and what is not, is the charge of the energy that imprinted it. Energy is charged with emotion. Since the subconscious has much conflicting information, the information that was charged with emotion is what comes up first. The conscious mind sorts through the information, and thinks thoughts that are formed by our deepest beliefs. It is not an instantaneous thing. Consequently, every thought doesn't manifest immediately.

If our thoughts manifest instantaneously we might see something like this. You think: "OK, if I can create whatever I want, I want a new Mercedes." Bingo, you got it. Actually, you would have to think, "I have created a new Mercedes." If you thought I want a Mercedes, that would indeed be your experience. You would just want one. But on to the rest of the story. Then you think, "I have now created a new mansion for myself, twenty-four rooms, etc." You got it. Then you decide to create twenty million dollars in your bank account. Bingo, you got it. Then you think, "Wow, this is too good to be true." Swish, away it all goes.

Fortunately it doesn't work that way. When you have a conscious thought, the subconscious checks its files to let you know if that thought coincides with its information. If it doesn't, you will most likely change the thought to be in harmony with the information stored in the subconscious, because that is your belief. Here on the conscious level you could consciously choose to change that belief, but it requires strength and determination. We will be looking at how we do this in upcoming chapters. Actually, most of our thoughts come to the conscious mind from the subconscious, so this would not occur. Our thoughts are almost automatically in sync with our beliefs.

One of the reasons that we are unable to understand how our beliefs create our experiences is because it happens in the time/space environment in which we live. The intellect (conscious and subconscious mind) is not capable of following this cause-and-effect relationship for the time necessary for its completion. It does not work in straight-line time, which is all the intellect understands.

We can, however, begin to see how this principle works by observing the thought patterns and experiences of others close to us. In time we will be able to see it in ourselves, but it is easier to observe it in others. This way we do not yet have to deal with the rationale of our own thinking.

People talk about the things they believe, and many times you will hear them say the same kinds of things over and over. An example would be: "I just can't seem to get ahead no matter what I do." You can also observe those beliefs showing up in their lives. You will notice that even when this person gets some extra money from some unexpected source, something always happens to use it up, like a car will break down or the washing machine will break. Whatever we believe on the deepest level of the subconscious will be true for us.

In one of our classes, it was interesting to observe from a class discussion how our beliefs differ, and produce the believed-in result. One participant was talking about his health problems, then others joined in to discuss health issues. Then another person said, "I can't relate to what you are talking about. I have never been sick a day in my life." Then he added, "But I sure have a hard time making any money." The one with health problems replied, "Making money is very easy for me, but I am sick a lot." When we start observing, it is easy to see how people create the experience of their beliefs.

Let's look at how cultural beliefs work. Back in the fourteenth century, almost everyone believed that the world was flat. Then Christopher Columbus had an intuitive awareness. It came to him that the world was round. Everyone said he was crazy. They all *knew* that the earth was flat, and that if you went too far out you would fall off. But as we know, he persuaded Queen Isabella to give him some ships so he could test his idea. His expedition proved that his intuitive inspiration was correct. What do you think his friends said when he returned? Did they say, "Bravo, Columbus, you proved us wrong," or did they say, "That can't be right." After all, these were intelligent people.

53

They had attended the universities, and all the professors taught them that the world was flat. Would they give up their beliefs that easily? Probably not. If Columbus could have persuaded them to sail around the world with him, they could have experienced for themselves the fact that the world was round. However, they still lived in a world where everyone else believed that it was flat. They would have lost their fear of falling off the earth, but they still lived in a society that lived in fear of falling off the earth.

Self-actualized people have figuratively sailed around the world. They know that life doesn't work the way most people believe it does. They have lost their fear of the unpredictable. They understand the laws of nature and how we all create our own experiences.

All new ideas come from the superconscious, intuitively. This is why we know that Columbus's idea that the world was round was an intuitive awareness. The subconscious can only give us information that has been programed into it. Every new discovery, every new invention, and what we call genius, all come to us as an intuitive inspiration from the superconscious. The superconscious is available to all of us if we make a choice to release the stress stored in our nervous systems and merge with our true selves. It is a matter of taking the time and doing whatever is necessary for us to become capable of discovering ourselves on a deeper level.

When we make a choice to heal the mind/body system, to take charge of our lives and change our beliefs, then we will discover that we are indeed Love expressing ourselves intelligently through energy. It is the stress stored in the system that also blocks our awareness of the Love. As the stress is released and the system gets stronger, we begin to experience Love on a very different level. We will know Love as the source of all creation, and the power of the universe. We are all a perfect expression of Love, Intelligence and Energy.

There is a process that we use for creating whatever we want in our lives. I want to give you an overview of this process here, then we will work through this process in Part Four.

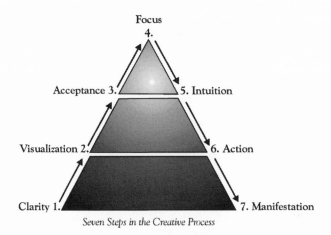

Seven Steps in the Creative Process

Step # 1 is **Clarity.** The first thing we need to establish is what we want. For many people it takes some time to get clear on exactly what they want. Remember, anything is possible, and all thought is creative. We will create whatever we focus our attention on; consequently, we want to be sure we know what we want to create as the first step in this process. Most of us have spent most of our lives simply reacting to what happened to us. Now that we understand that we are creating whatever we experience, it is time to start creating consciously. If we do not get clear on what we want, we will create whatever the subconscious believes in.

Step # 2 is **Visualization.** Sometimes people tell me that they do not know how to visualize. They are mistaken. They just do not know that they know how to visualize. We all do it all the time. If I say to you, "Do not picture a pink cow in your mind," what happens? You visualize a pink cow. Visualization is a part of imagination. You can't keep from doing it.

A visual image creates a form in mind. This form attracts the energy necessary to fill it. When this process is completed, whatever we are visualizing manifests in the material world. Of course, everything we visualize does not manifest. There are some other criteria for manifestation, which brings us to the next step.

Step # 3 is **Acceptance**. Acceptance is the most difficult step for most people. You might be thinking, "Why wouldn't I accept what I want?" This is where our beliefs come in. Remember that about eighty-five percent of what we believe is not on the conscious level. Therefore, we are not aware of many of our beliefs. In order to work through the acceptance step, we must become conscious of our beliefs. If our beliefs do not support our visions, we must change them in order to create what we want. Our visions cannot be manifested in the material world until we have accepted them in our minds.

Step # 4 is **Focusing Attention**. Whatever we focus our attention on is what we attract into our lives. So, there are two areas we need to understand about focusing attention. First is going back to Step # 1. We need to be clear about what we want to create. We tend to focus our attention on our problems, thus creating more problems. Focusing our attention on something automatically attracts the energy that matches whatever we are focusing on. If we believe we have a problem, when we focus our attention on it, we simply attract more energy to perpetuate the problem. Experiences must have energy to exist and they get that energy by our focusing attention on them. The best way to alleviate a problem is to stop giving it any attention and it will go away. We need to focus our attention on what we want to create instead of on our problems.

The second area we need to understand about focusing attention is our ability to focus. When the nervous system is overstressed, it becomes increasingly difficult to focus our attention on what we want. It invariably wanders off onto the problem or onto other things, which usually include fears and doubts. As the nervous system becomes stronger, our perception becomes clearer, and we are able to see possibilities. Fear and doubt fade away. Once we are strong enough to focus our attention on what we want in a very powerful way, things start to happen much faster. This is the reason why focusing attention is the capstone on our chart of the seven steps in the creative process. Once we are able to powerfully focus our attention, the remainder of the process is downhill.

Step # 5 is **Intuitive Inspiration**. Once the nervous system releases a sufficient amount of stress, the mind/body energy becomes more refined, which automatically puts us in touch with intuitive awareness. Intuitive inspiration is always there for us, but much of the time we are not capable of tuning in to it. When our energy has become sufficiently refined so that it can vibrate in harmony with the superconscious, the only thing we have to do is listen. We must become conscious that it is there for us and listen for its guidance.

The way we learn to listen to our intuition is by stilling the intellect. We must teach the thinking aspect of our minds to settle down. Our thoughts are going constantly, and we cannot hear our intuition as long as our thoughts are demanding all of our attention. In order to tap into the intuitive mind, we can teach the thinking mind to focus on one point. Once the conscious mind is focused on one point, it settles down and automatically merges the conscious mind with the superconscious. This is the level of all knowledge. Each time we merge the conscious mind with the superconscious, we return with expanded awareness. This is how we open the path for intuitive awareness to flow into the conscious mind.

This process is called meditation. When we meditate on a regular basis, we open the channel for intuitive inspiration to flow into the conscious mind whenever it is needed. When we have a question, we simply ask. We go into meditation, and the answer will soon appear. It comes in many different ways. Once we learn that the answers will come and we begin to expect them, they come quite automatically. We will work with techniques for preparing ourselves to be capable of receiving intuitive guidance in Part Four

The fifth step is to listen to our intuitive inspiration for what we need to do to manifest our vision.

Step # 6 is **Action**. This part is easy when we have worked through the other five steps. We simply follow through with whatever comes to us. The action step cannot be overlooked. However, since it is the closest to the manifestation, we think it is the most important. Action without the other five steps in preparation for it is usually ineffective. We usually go from a vague idea of what we want right into action. If we work hard enough, and long enough, we will get some results, but they may not be the desired results. Even if you get the desired results, it is the hard way to go.

Step # 7 is **Manifestation**. When we follow the previous six steps, manifestation is automatic. It probably shouldn't even be considered a step since it is actually the result of following the other steps. However, it is important that we recognize it as a part of the process. By the time we have created what we wanted, we can easily overlook the fact that we actually created it. If we are aware and we observe the entire process, it becomes much easier to understand exactly how we create, and how we can create whatever we want.

There is one other thing that we want to touch upon here that plays a major role in understanding how we can create our visions in the fastest and most effective way possible, and that is meditation.

Meditation

In Part Four I will give you some guidelines for learning how to meditate, but here I want you to know how it works in manifesting our visions.

Meditation is a process that is accomplished by bringing the body and mind to a point of stillness and silence. When we accomplish this, the conscious mind merges with the superconscious, which is all intelligence. This is the level of all possibilities. This is what we call universal intelligence, an aspect of the source. This is the level where all of creation is created. On the level of the source, energy has not yet been formed. Since this is the level of stillness and silence, we are unable to think on this level. However, the most powerful thoughts we can have for manifesting our desires are as close as possible to this level. Once the mind moves (thinks), energy is created. Then we can give form to that energy by bringing into our consciousness whatever we want to create. In Part Four we will have specific guidelines for how to do this.

It's All About Choice

*Destiny is not a matter of chance, it is a matter of choice;
it is not a thing to be waited for, it is a thing to be
achieved.*—William Jennings Bryan

The seventh law of nature, discussed in chapter 5, states: **We all make our own choices.** We make choices that coincide with our beliefs. Every choice has a consequence; that is how our experiences come to be. Even if we choose not to choose, we have still made a choice, and we will still experience the consequence of that choice.

This law of nature guarantees us the power to take charge of our lives, and create them the way we choose. Many times we cannot see a choice that we believe will bring about our desired result. In this case, we usually say, "I have no choice." Since we are an expression of universal intelligence, we always have choices. There are infinite choices possible, but we may not be able to see them at any given time. The two things that block our ability to see possibilities are the stress that keeps the nervous system from functioning as it is designed to function and our deep-seated beliefs.

When we find ourselves in a situation where we cannot see any possibilities that would fulfill our desires, we need to get some rest, do the program that is provided in Part Four, and question our beliefs. Anything is possible, but it is our beliefs that limit us. Again, we need to remember that beliefs are just information that we have accepted as true. When we are able to see our beliefs from a different perspective, we begin to realize that they are not necessarily true, and that we can change them.

Since the seven laws of nature are governing our lives, we are all born with the innate ability to create the life we want for ourselves. The reason we are unaware of this is because we do not know who we are. When we choose to follow the program laid out in Part Four on a daily basis, we discover who we are. We will all discover, with practice over time, that we are at one with all power. We are not separate entities, but we are all Love, intelligence and energy. There is nothing else in existence, therefore nothing is separate from us.

We discover that our desires and the fulfillment of our desires come from the same source. There is nothing wrong with our desires. The problems arise from the means we use to fulfill them. Our problems are a result of either our inability to fulfill our desires, or our lack of understanding of how to fulfill our desires. Since our desires and the fulfillment of our desires come from the same source, all we need to do is bring our conscious awareness to the level of the Source, which contains all intelligence, and we can intuitively know how to make choices that will produce the desired result.

Again let's look at why we do not know the power that lies dormant within each of us. Our physical bodies, including our nervous systems, are capable of handling only a limited amount of stress. Let's look at what happens when the system can no longer function properly, and the stress keeps coming.

This happens many times with children as well as adults. Children are trying to learn how the world works, and how to fit into it, without yet being fully developed. Due to their inability to understand, children can be very cruel.

I will never forget an incident that I experienced in grade school. I was returning to class from recess when I came upon a group of fifteen or twenty children who had cornered a little girl and were verbally assaulting her. The victim came from a very poor family. Her clothes were ragged, and she was not blessed with natural beauty. These children were calling her terrible names such as "scarecrow." My heart went out to her. I was enraged that they were treating her in such a manner, but I did nothing about it. I simply walked by without saying anything. For years I felt guilty about not standing up for her, but I didn't, because I couldn't. I did not believe that I could make a difference, and I was afraid that if I said anything they would start being nasty to me as well. My choice was one of self-preservation, but not an admirable one to me at the time.

Can you imagine the stress this situation caused this little girl? I am sure there were also many other stressful situations in her life. What happens when a child's or an adult's nervous system cannot handle it any more? They either have a nervous breakdown or they turn to violence. They can't help it, one or the other is inevitable or maybe both. Actually, becoming violent is a characteristic of a nervous system breakdown.

Many children learn to endure this kind of stress. In many cases their poor self-image is due to the kind of family life they have. The beliefs of their families and people they associate with form their beliefs about themselves. Does this mean that this child, or any other child that survives abuse, is doomed to a life of misery? Absolutely not!

All of us, no matter what age, have the power within ourselves to change our lives. It may not be easy, but anyone who reads this book can begin working with the process laid out in Part Four, and start releasing the stress that has been stored in the nervous system. Then they will discover their own inner power to create the kind of life they want. For most people, it is a process over time, but it can be done. The condition of our nervous system determines our ability to see possibilities and to make choices that work for us.

Let's now take a look at how energy is always working in our lives. Whatever we do, say, or believe is always putting out an energy. Due to the law of attraction and repulsion, this energy demands that like energy is returned. When someone smiles at us, we usually smile back, right? If someone is nasty to us, our natural reaction is to be nasty right back to them. However, we do have a choice. If we are strong enough to be con-

scious of what is happening, we can choose to react in a different manner. We could simply ask, "What's wrong with you today?" If we can move beyond the demand of the energy, and
simply not buy into it, we can control how someone else's energy affects us.

How we feel or what we believe about ourselves is also constantly creating an energy field around us that demands that
others respond in like manner. If we believe that we are ugly,
stupid or useless, others will tend to accept that belief about us.
On the other hand, since beliefs are simply information that we
have accepted as true, we can choose to believe something quite
different from what we have heard in the past. This, of course,
requires a strong nervous system. If we are strong enough, and
someone says to us, "I think you are stupid!" we can sidestep
that energy, and say to ourself, "I disagree. I think I am brilliant." Most of these things are not usually said out loud, but
work more on the level of thought. When we choose to release
the stress stored in our nervous systems and create a strong
positive self-image, we find people will respond to us with respect. Generally, other people will see us the way we see ourselves. It is an automatic and unconscious response.

Let's look at my particular situation. I was very fortunate
in having a very loving family. My mother saw to it that I ate
good nutritious food and everyone in my environment treated
me well. I was exposed to some very good beliefs, one of which
was that I could accomplish whatever I chose to do. This background gave me a certain amount of confidence. It gave me
enough confidence to automatically receive the respect of the
other children around me, but still not enough to push my
luck by defending someone who was not popular. Even under
the best of circumstances, growing up is stressful. We need to
do everything possible to help our children feel good about
themselves.

Many adults are still carrying the stress that was created
while they were growing up. Think about your childhood and
teen years. If this thought or remembrance stirs an emotional
reaction in you, then this stress is still stored in your nervous

system. You can let it go through the practice of the process laid out in Part Four, and your conscious realization that it is over. It doesn't matter any more, and you can choose to let it go. You can check your success some time later by bringing the incident back to consciousness and checking your feelings about it.

This brings us to another very important point that we need to understand. It is the other side of the principle that says, we all make our own choices. This principle is that *you cannot make choices for others.* Laws of nature or principles of life guarantee that we each can choose for ourselves, thereby giving us the power to create whatever we choose, but we must remember that everyone else also has that privilege. For example, we cannot change someone else. We can choose to have a happy, harmonious marriage, and we can even choose the characteristics of our partner. But we cannot choose that a particular person fit a profile that we created, or that a certain person wants to be with us. When we are working with creating what we want, and we get clear about what the special person in our life will be like, we have for all practical purposes put in our order. Universal intelligence will deliver whatever we ordered, but it will be a person who also wants someone like us. It could be someone we already know or someone entirely new to us. We all get to make our own choices, so we need to be sure that we understand this.

My husband, Dean, tells a story of a time when he was in the U.S. Navy. He and a black soldier, who was well decorated for his contributions in the war, were boarding a bus somewhere in the South during a time when buses were segregated. The driver told the black soldier to go to the back of the bus, but there weren't any seats left in the black section, so the driver said the soldier would have to get off. Dean told the driver that there was an empty seat next to him, and that the black soldier should be able to sit there. He demanded that the black soldier be able to stay on the bus. He explained what this black soldier had done for his country, and said he deserved to ride this bus if anyone did. Before he even knew what was happening, Dean found himself being bodily taken off the bus and set on the curb of the street. The black soldier was sitting by him. The black soldier looked at him and asked, "Where are you from, sir?" Then he explained to Dean that you do not do things like that down here.

Dean saw injustice and was strong enough to try to make a difference, which was admirable, but he was trying to make a choice for someone else, which didn't work. The principles of life provide us with a means for creating the life we want for ourselves, but no one else can do it for us. We can create our personal life the way we want it to be, but can we eliminate injustice? No. We can choose not to participate in it, but someone else has chosen to create it, which is simply a matter of the law working the way it works.

We will all encounter obstacles on our path to accomplishing whatever we choose to do, whether it is taking a bus across town or other more important things. We then look at the situation and make a choice about how to handle it.

A friend of mine has written a book titled *A Woman Can Do That!* The book is a guide to help women overcome discrimination and achieve success in the workplace. She interviewed me along with a number of other women, and one of the questions she asked me was how I handled the discrimination issue. I told her that my first choice was to avoid it whenever possible. This is an example of another roadblock that keeps showing up on our journeys. My choice is always to simply go around it if possible.

After a very short career in the corporate world of bosses and employees, I realized that this was not the place for me. I needed to be an entrepreneur, and I have been one ever since. I still run into discrimination occasionally, but I simply ignore it. A problem can only exist in our lives if we give it energy by focusing our attention on it. If we refuse to pay any attention to a problem, in time it will vanish. Remember that everything in existence is energy, and we give energy to something by focusing our attention on it.

You could also think of it in relationship to the law of giving . . . and receiving. Giving and receiving are two sides of the same coin; you can't have one without the other. Someone is using his right to make choices, and has done so by creating discrimination against women, or anyone else for that matter. It is a "gift" someone wants to give me, but I am not accepting it. Consequently, nothing is happening. Nothing can be given without a receiver, or received without a giver. This law also supports nature's perfect order of making each of us in charge of our own lives. We get to choose what we give, and we get to choose what we receive.

The reason we have not discovered the power we have within ourselves is because we have always focused our attention outward. We believe that others have all the power and that they can make life good or miserable for us. This belief, however, has not served us well. Here we are now discovering that all the power there is is centered within us. This requires a change in belief and a change in focus. When we want to do something good, it usually means changing the world. So we go out there and try to make choices for other people, and usually make little progress. If we want to change the world, we must start with ourselves. All of the power is right within us, but it only works to create whatever we want in our lives. However, if we see ourselves living in an orderly compassionate world, that vision puts out an energy that demands a response.

Let's take a look now at how important it is for us to stay focused on our own self-interest. The universe is set up to function perfectly if we all do this. In fact, our own self-interest is really all we truly know. When we try to think of others before ourselves, this is a form of trying to make choices for other people. The system is perfect. We just need to understand how it works.

This reminds me of a time when I was single and living in an apartment building in Minneapolis. There was a really nice guy who also lived in my building. We saw each other at parties, and had talked. I knew he liked me and would in time ask me out. I was also very impressed with him. At one of the building parties we were talking and discovered that we were both going to be in Chicago on business trips the following week. Neither of us knew anyone there, so we decided we would both stay for the weekend and do some things together there. I was really looking forward to my weekend date. Since I didn't know him well, I really didn't know what kind of things he liked to do, so I decided to just let him make the decisions about what we did. He also was determined to make a good impression with me, so he made the same decision. The weekend was a disaster. He would ask, "Where would you like to go for dinner?" I would reply, "Wherever you would like to go would be fine with me." This kind of conversation was carried out by each of us. We both tried so hard to please the other that we were both exhausted by the end of the weekend, and after returning home, never dated each other again.

Had we both functioned from our own self-interest, we might have gotten to know each other, and who knows, we might even have liked each other. But since neither of us did, we had an uncomfortable weekend, and we lost our opportunity to at least get to know each other.

We can never know what is best for someone else, but if we take care of creating what is best for us, universal intelligence will take care of everything else. What is truly good for any of us will turn out to be good for everyone concerned. Universal intelligence knows how to take care of that, even though everyone involved may not be able to see it clearly at a given time. If we can remember that we are all connected, our separateness is only in form, then we can understand how this perfect system takes care of everyone if we just take care of our own business.

I do not mean to imply, in any way, that we do not care about, or give consideration to, the welfare and feelings of other people. As our nervous systems become stronger, we simply begin to see and understand the perfect order in everything. Universal intelligence clearly has it all under control. When we know who we are, and that we are not separate from anyone else, our choices are always coming from a desire to bring about the greatest good possible for everyone. It is just that we are the only one whose life we are creating, and acting from our own level of knowledge and self-interest works perfectly.

Once we begin to focus our attention inward and we discover the power we have to create, as well as the perfection of the system in which we live, we learn to relax and go with the flow. Once we make the choice to live our lives consciously, life takes on a totally different flavor. We learn the value of nonresistance. We stop trying to make choices for other people, and begin to be willing to simply experience whatever is. Since we know there is a reason for whatever is, we do not need to control it. When we are willing to let go of resistance and simply experience, we begin to understand the true nature of life. We can be conscious in the present and know that all is well.

Next let's think about creating optimal health.

Creating Optimal Health

... within man is the soul of the whole; the wise silence;
the universal beauty of which every part and particle is
equally related; the eternal One.—Ralph Waldo Emerson

We want to look at our mind/body system from a somewhat different perspective than what we usually think of when we think about creating health. Our senses tell us that our bodies are solid. However, many years ago Einstein proved that everything in existence is energy. Consequently, we know that the entire mind/body system is energy and intelligence. It is, in fact, an electromagnetic energy field expressing itself in a certain form. All energy is intelligent; therefore, the energy that makes up the mind/body system has its own intelligence.

Today's new science, quantum physics, sees the world made up of vibrations and energy waves. The smallest particle of matter is called "quantum." Einstein's equation $E=MC^2$ states that there is no true distinction between energy and matter. One centimeter contains one hundred million atoms.

The nucleus accounts for almost all the atom's solidity, yet occupies only one-million-millionth of its total volume; the rest is empty space. What is this empty space? Physicists are now calling it a field of intelligence.

This atomic structure is not mass, but energy. For example, the cells in the body vibrate at about a thousand times per second; molecules vibrate at a million times per second; atoms vibrate at a quadrillion times per second. This gives our bodies and the world around us the appearance of being solid.

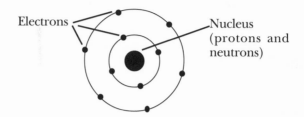

We cannot perceive this because our five physical senses are not sensitive to the levels of light that come from the vibrating particles. If they were, we could see through the vibrating particles and they would not appear solid to us. We have equipment to measure energy waves which we cannot see, such as gamma rays, X rays, ultraviolet rays, infrared rays and radio waves. Our senses can detect only a fraction of the measurable energy known to us.

On the level of the Source, energy is highly refined. As the energy waves get longer they become more dense. When they get dense enough, they appear to the senses to be matter.

Now with the understanding that we are really not solid, but energy, let's look at how we work with this energy to create optimal health. Health, therefore, means the free flow of energy, with its intelligence intact, throughout the entire mind/body system. We could also conclude that illness or malfunction would be the result of the blockage of the free flow of energy.

As we know, energy vibrates at different levels of density. Let's take a look at the different levels of energy within ourselves.

The energy of the physical body is dense enough for us to see it. The conscious mind is comprised of a more refined energy and cannot be seen. The subconscious mind is more refined than the conscious mind, and our feeling level is still more refined. Our center, our source, our inner being is the most highly refined energy possible. We can understand energy in terms of density and refinement or faster vibrations and slower

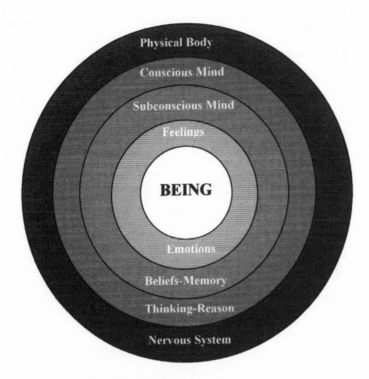

vibrations. We can also think of the vibrations as heavy or light. The slower, denser, heavier energy appears more solid.

This is what optimal health is all about. It is about the perfect connection between body, mind, emotions and spirit. In order to know who we are on the level of Being (Spirit), the energy of the entire body/mind system must become more refined for it to connect with the highly refined energy of our own inner being. In Part Four, I provide a process for refining the energy of the mind/body system which makes it possible for us to know ourselves on the level of the superconscious or the source (Being). When the mind/body system reaches this vibratory level, we have accomplished optimal health and self-actualization. We are then capable of perfect health, intuitive guidance and creating the lives we want for ourselves.

Next, let's look at how our mind/body energy relates to the world around us. Since everything in existence is energy, and interrelated, every aspect of the mind/body system is affected by the energy around us.

When we think of creating optimal health we usually think of diet and nutrition. When looking at creating health on the energy level, we know that food is also energy. There are many good books on nutrition, and also much confusion, but what I want to say here is that we need to understand that the energy of the food we eat can contribute only the energy that it has. Consequently, it is important to eat the freshest food possible.

Another thing that is important in choosing our food is the awareness of our body's intelligence. If we are willing to experiment and to be observant, our body will tell us what it needs. We need to trust our body's intelligence. Our bodies are as different and unique as our personalities. What works for one does not necessarily work for another. By eating according to what others say is good for us, we are actually giving away our power.

To give you an example of the body's intelligence, I would like to share with you an experiment that my father-in-law tried. He owned a large chicken hatchery, and was always concerned with the best food for his chickens. He tried many different formulas because he knew they needed certain nutrients in order to produce the most eggs. Then one day it occurred to him that the chickens would know how to eat best for themselves if they were given a choice. In separate containers he provided all the different foods, vitamins, and minerals known to be good for chickens. Then he let them eat whatever they wanted. The results were amazing. The chickens did not all eat the same thing, but they did begin to lay far more eggs than other chickens. The method became quite popular and was known as the free choice feeding method. He gained a great deal of recognition for his amazing discovery.

Have you ever noticed how your body feels after eating a meal that does not contain the nutrients that it needs? What I notice is that I feel full, but not satisfied. I still want something else to eat even though I do not want to eat more. Our bodies are highly intelligent, and we are greatly benefited by becoming aware of this intelligence.

In order to create optimal health, we will work with all levels of energy, the seen and the unseen.

In Part Four you will be given instructions for exercising all areas of the body. These exercises work with the energy that make up the body/mind system. First we will look at the endocrine glands. These glands secrete hormones directly into the bloodstream, and they all interact with each other. Their development and functioning are of great importance to our well-being. The hormones they secrete are responsible for the differences between a small person and a large person, a genius or someone of low intelligence, and the difference between a happy person or cheerless individual. They are responsible for our energy, activity, radiance, and stability, as well as the vitalization of the life processes. Their influence is pervasive in all that we do and all that we are. They are responsible for determining the forms of our bodies and the workings of our minds. Each of these glands needs to be exercised or stimulated on a regular basis in order to create optimal health.

In the same areas of the body as the endocrine glands we also have unseen energy centers that lie dormant unless we activate them. The set of exercises in Part Four will stimulate the endocrine glands, allowing them to function at their highest level. They will also activate the energy centers, releasing a much greater supply of energy for creating health throughout the entire body/mind system. These exercises also keep the entire body flexible, and release stress that is stored in the nervous system. They refine the energy of the entire system and prepare the body for meditation which allows the conscious mind to merge with the superconscious. This is how we develop our intuitive abilities and discover the spiritual essence that is who we are.

Psychological Health

The book club in the community where I live read *The End of the Affair* by Graham Greene, a perfect case study of how our energy and beliefs determine our experiences. Bendrix, the man in the affair, was very jealous. Jealousy is a result of low self-esteem. When we feel inferior, inadequate, undesirable, or do not feel good about ourselves, we have judged ourselves according to our beliefs, and that energy creates our experiences. Sarah, a beautiful woman, fell in love with Bendrix. Due to his low self-esteem, Bendrix believed that he did not deserve someone this beautiful and that she would surely leave him.

What we are all doing, at every moment, is creating lives that match our beliefs. Consequently, Bendrix sabotaged the relationship. With his jealousy and fear, he created an atmosphere that would cause his lover to leave him. Sarah loved him very much, but they were constantly arguing because of his insecurity. When she did leave he was devastated, but also relieved. This returned the equilibrium to his life. His life again matched his beliefs.

Unfortunately, thousands of people are living their lives in this same catch-22 situation. Our lives must match whatever we believe, and we will do whatever is necessary to bring that about.

If you are in a relationship with someone who has low self-esteem there is nothing that you can do to change it. No matter how great you think this person is, it is what he/she thinks that runs their lives, and in all probability you will not be able to change his/her mind.

The reason it is so hard for us to change our beliefs is because our beliefs are also energy and are integrated into the mind/body energy field. In order to change our beliefs we must work with each part of the entire mind/body energy field simultaneously. This is why we must create a new lifestyle in order to create optimal health on all levels—physical, mental, emotional and spiritual.

When we begin to release the stress built up in the nervous system and refine the energy within the system so that we are capable of bringing the conscious mind to merge with the superconscious, then we become aware of who we really are. Then we begin to know ourselves as whole, complete, perfect and powerful. Once we expand our awareness to know ourselves on a deeper level, how could we possibly entertain thoughts about ourselves that would see us as inferior, inadequate or undesirable. We then know ourselves as Love, joy, beauty, intelligence, strength, power, whole, complete and perfect. When we are able to do this we then know everyone else is also this wholeness. We are never inferior or superior. We are all perfect expressions of this one source.

Sarah, the woman in Greene's book, was married, but there was no intimacy in her marriage. Consequently, she felt that something important to her happiness was missing. She longed for an intimate relationship, which she found with Bendrix.

When we feel that something is missing in our lives, there is an energy that emanates from us that announces that we are searching or open for that emptiness to be filled, and what we feel we need is evident. This energy automatically came from Sarah, and the men she met responded to it.

Have you ever noticed this kind of energy coming from someone? If we are observant we can feel the energy that we all automatically put out that tells the world what is missing in our lives.

Both Bendrix and Sarah had something else missing in their lives. They needed spiritual understanding. They both felt very incomplete and longed for some sense of meaning or understanding of life. They could not believe the traditional thinking about God. Consequently, they denied the existence of God. They could see the evidence that there has to be some power that governs and makes possible all the things we experience. Yet neither of them could understand it. Bendrix handled his frustration by simply denying the existence of God regardless of the evidence. Sarah could not continue to deny the existence of a higher power, so she tried to find the answer by going to church. This added more conflicting beliefs in her thinking, which made her life even more unbearable.

We are programed to look to someone else for the answers to our questions. So naturally Sarah believed that she should go to a religious organization to learn about God. Whether we go to a priest, rabbi, minister or a counselor, they will tell us about their beliefs or the accepted beliefs of the organization. Remember, **all beliefs are simply information that has been accepted as truth.** This counseling may or may not be beneficial, but finding God is an inner process, not an outer one.

In part IV I lay out a process for releasing the stress that blocks our ability to go within, refine the body/mind energy, and give you techniques for meditation, which is how we become aware of who we are and our Source.

All of us need to have meaning in our lives. We need to have some kind of experience that lets us know that there is universal order and that we are a part of it. As we work with this process for creating optimal health, we will discover our source and the source of all creation right within ourselves.

In order to create the lives we want for ourselves we must start by creating optimal health. This more refined way of functioning gives us the ability to take charge of our lives and create whatever we choose.

Living in Harmony **10** with the Principles of Life

Mind moves matter.—Virgil, first century poet

Here we want to take a look at how life works, governed by basic, nonchanging principles or laws of nature, and how we create our own experiences. It will be clear to see how we can create the lives we want for ourselves by living in harmony with these principles.

The first principle we discovered is that **everything in existence is Love expressing intelligently through energy.** This principle is the basis of our existence. It tells us that we are not separate entities, that we are all expressions of the one source (Love/God) that is the source of all of existence. We are at one with all love, all intelligence and all energy. It helps us to understand that the fulfillment of our desires is not an external process. Our desires and the fulfillment of our desires come from the same source. The only way we can keep from fulfilling our desires is by overstressing the mind/body system to where it is not capable of perceiving this principle or knowing its own inner self. What we will discover is that we can connect with all the power that exists right within ourselves.

Next let's look at our second principle, which shows us how we create our experiences. The second principle is that **thought directs energy, or mind energy directs physical energy.** There is a phrase in the Bible in Philippians 4:8, which

77

states, "Finally, brethren, whatsoever things are true, whatsoever things are honest, whatsoever things are just, whatsoever things are pure, whatsoever things are lovely, whatsoever things are of good report; if there be any virtue, and if there be any praise, think on these things." These were instructions on how to live successfully. Why should we focus our attention only on the good? Because whatever we focus our attention on is what we will attract into our lives.

My mother was a very religious person, and she brought me to church every time the doors opened. But what I heard confused me. They said if I wanted to be saved, that I must believe. My questions were: "Saved from what? What do I need to believe?" The answers I got then didn't help me any, but now that I understand this principle that thought or belief directs energy, it is clear to see that what we all need to believe in is whatever we want to create. Because whatever we do believe in is what we will create. And if we understand this, we will be saved from much confusion and disappointment.

This principle that thought or beliefs direct energy puts us all in direct control of our own experiences. Since everything is energy, and thought directs and forms energy, this is how we create the experiences in our lives. Unfortunately, most of our beliefs have simply been programed into our thinking by the people around us and the environment we live in. Most people have never taken the time to observe their beliefs, or to question them to see if they are producing the desired results. The reason for this, of course, is because most people are unaware of this principle, and do not realize that we are creating our own experiences through our own beliefs and thought patterns. Once we understand this principle we can become conscious about our beliefs and change the ones that do not serve us well. It is my experience that this is a process over time, but well worth the effort. In Part Four I will give you some more guidelines for working with a process that will make it possible for you to take charge of your life and work in harmony with this principle.

Two of the other principles that are important to consider here are that **beliefs are simply information that we have ac-**

cepted as truth, and that **everything in the relative world is always changing**. These principles again guarantee that we are in charge of our own lives. What makes a belief true for us is our own perception. What is true for us is whatever we believe it to be. I am sure we have all heard two people, who had the same experience, describe it in totally opposite ways. For example, the experience of losing a job. Many times several people lose their jobs at the same time. One person will be totally devastated, filled with fear and uncertainty, while another will feel exhilarated and excited about the prospects for the future. How we react to any situation is determined by our own thoughts and beliefs, or in other words, the things we say to ourselves. If we believe all things work together for good, whatever the situation is we look for the good in it. And guess what? We usually find it. If we believe we are losers, and nothing ever works out right for us, that will be our experience.

The exciting thing is that we can change our beliefs and our experiences will change accordingly. We can learn how to live in harmony with these principles and create whatever we want.

The next principle we want to look at is **the law of attraction and repulsion**, or **what comes from us returns to us.** This law guarantees that whatever we can create in our minds, we can create in our experiences. It works in a very automatic way, as all laws of nature do. All of our thoughts are affected by this principle. Thoughts are mental energy, and they attract to themselves the energy necessary to fulfill our visions or expectations. Consequently, we want to keep our thoughts focused on the kind of things we want to experience.

By now you are probably saying, "Wait a minute. I have experienced many things that I had never thought about or expected would ever happen to me." First let's remember that most of our beliefs are not on the conscious level. But in addition, certain things will simply come up in our lives for our growth. Eastern philosophy relates most of these things to what is called karma, or the reaction to your actions in a previous life. Whether you believe in karma or previous lifetimes is irrelevant. It suffices to say that we will each face certain challenges, or what appear to be unfortunate situations, in our life. We may have never thought of the occurrence, but we do have choices about how we deal with it. This brings us to the next principle we want to consider—that **we all make our own choices.**

Now is the only time in existence, so whatever is now is what we must deal with. It doesn't change anything to whine, complain or wish things were different. The only way we can grow or change anything is to make choices about what is. If we don't like what is, for the most part we can change it. But that is a process over time. There are, of course, some things that are not changeable. An example of this might be the death of someone close to you. We cannot change the occurrence, but we can choose how we react to it. Whatever the situation, we always have choices, and our choices will always relate to our beliefs. If we know we have choices, and can make things different or better, we deal with whatever is in a constructive way. This principle again gives us the power to create the lives we want for ourselves.

The last principle we want to look at is that **giving and receiving are two sides of the same coin.** All of these principles have given us everything we need to create whatever we want. However, in order for anything to happen, the circle must be completed. We must be willing and capable of receiving our desires. We again get to choose. We do not have to receive anything that we do not want, nor do we have to give anything that we do not want to give. When we learn how to fully accept only good in our lives, it is only good that we have to give, and everyone gets to choose what they will accept.

It is easy to see that we can create magnificent lives for ourselves if we choose to do so.

In summary, here are the seven laws of nature or principles of life, that are governing how we create our experiences:

1. **Everything in existence is Love expressing intelligently through energy.**
2. **Thought (belief) directs energy.**

3. **Beliefs are simply information that we have accepted as truth.**

4. **Everything in the relative world is always changing.**

5. **The law of attraction and repulsion: What comes from us returns to us.**

6. **We all make our own choices.**

7. **Giving and receiving are two sides of the same coin.**

In the next section we will look at how different all areas of life could be if we choose to make the commitment to take charge of our lives and create a new way of living.

Part Three

What's the Difference?

Introduction

In this section we want to see what difference it would make in all areas of our lives if we became self-actualized. I will use the word "ordinary" to describe the person who is functioning with the use of only the intellect and the five senses, which is true for the majority of us.

The self-actualized person has the intellect and senses just as the ordinary person, but they also have the ability to tap into what I call the fourth dimension, or the spiritual dimension, of life. Knowledge from this dimension is brought to the conscious mind through intuition. From this level of knowledge we are able to perceive the laws of nature that govern our lives and the material world. Therefore, the self-actualized person will see any situation from a different perspective than the ordinary person, and consequently will act in a different way.

Each chapter in this section will explain the differences in one area of life. I will select situations that I believe are common to most of us in our personal lives, in our relationships, in business or the workplace. Then in the last chapter we will look at how our society could change as more and more of us become self-actualized.

What's the Difference 11 in Personal Experiences?

In as much as the Soul is present, there will be power.—
Ralph Waldo Emerson

Subject: Self Image

How do you feel about yourself? For the ordinary person, how we feel about ourselves is determined primarily by what other people think about us, or the feedback we get from others. The ordinary person allows other people to affect his perception, and needs the approval of others in order to feel good about himself.

The self-actualized person enjoys the approval of others, but does not need it in order to feel good about himself. He understands that we are all connected, and that it is our own thinking that determines how others respond to us. He knows that everything is energy, and that his thoughts are subject to the law of attraction and repulsion. It is his thoughts about himself that determine what others think about him.

Subject: Time

Do you have enough time? The ordinary person believes that time is limited, and usually feels pressure and anxiety about getting things done in a specific time frame.

The self-actualized person knows that time is eternal. There are twenty-four hours in every day for each of us. He realizes that it is he who has created the time frames in his life. And if he has created something that doesn't work well for him, he can create different time frames or different expectations. He realizes that it is his thoughts and beliefs that have created the situations he finds himself in, and he can change his thoughts or choices to create something different. The self-actualized person knows that he is in charge of his life and it is up to him to create whatever he wants.

Subject: Survival or Work

Do you work to survive? How do you feel about your work? The ordinary person believes that he must work to survive. He must work in order to make the money necessary to fulfill his needs. In this case, the amount of money a specific job pays is a major factor in determining what one does. When the ordinary person is out of work, he probably will feel a great deal of stress and anxiety.

The self-actualized person works just as the ordinary person does. However, he does not believe that his work is essential to his survival. He knows that he is a part of a perfect system that puts him in the right place, at the right time, in order to fulfill his purpose in being here. He knows that we are all parts of a perfect system, and are guided by universal intelligence to bring about whatever is necessary for the growth and fulfillment of the whole. He sees his work as an opportunity to express himself. He knows that his desires and the fulfillment of his desires come from the same source; consequently, he cannot have a desire without the means to fulfill it. He trusts this universal intelligence; therefore, he is relatively unaffected by being out of work. He sees being out of work as an opportunity to move on to something else which will bring him greater growth and fulfillment.

The self-actualized person's work is usually something he enjoys doing. He knows that thought directs energy; therefore, he expects to do work that he enjoys. In fact he expects only good experiences to come into his life. Since we usually find what we are looking for, even if the experience such as losing a job seems to be negative, the self-actualized person sees it as positive, and it usually is.

Subject: Money

Do you have enough money? The ordinary person believes that he must make money to provide for his needs. For most there is never quite enough money to fulfill all desires. This keeps us motivated to keep working harder to accumulate money. Many times the ordinary person is not clear about what money really is, or its real value. There is just this underlying feeling that more is better.

The self-actualized person knows that money is simply a means of exchange. He does not feel compelled to make money. He knows that money is a form of energy, as is everything in existence. He also knows that thought directs energy; therefore, thinking is a precursor to acting. He understands the law of attraction and repulsion, and knows that he can attract the money he needs when his thinking is clear and focused. This does not mean that he does not work; it simply means he sees the situation from a different perspective. The self-actualized person is capable of creating the money he needs to serve his purpose, or fulfill his desires. Some self-actualized people have large amounts of money, while others have very little. How much one creates is determined by the amount of money needed for what one wants to do. The self-actualized person has a much better understanding of what money is and how it works than does the ordinary person.

Subject: Judgment of others

Do you often judge other people and have strong opinions about the appropriateness of events and circumstances that do not involve you? The ordinary person likes to judge other people. He thinks that whatever amount of information he has about another person or event is sufficient to make a judgment about it. As we discussed before, the intellect can only see parts, or gather incomplete information. It cannot see the big picture or how all the parts fit together. But when we have only the senses and intellect to work with, our intellect believes it knows everything necessary to make a judgment, and it does so.

The self-actualized person knows that the intellect is limited. It is incapable of having all the information necessary to make a judgment about another person or event. Therefore the self-actualized person simply accepts whatever he sees, and doesn't bother to judge it. He realizes that he doesn't have the information necessary to make a fair or accurate judgment.

Subject: Anger

Do you anger easily? How do you express your anger? The ordinary person sees other people as totally separate from himself. When someone does something that seems threatening to us we usually become angry. If we think someone is infringing on our rights, it provokes anger. For example, how do you feel when someone in the car behind you blows his horn the second the light turns or follows too close behind you or cuts in front of you? For many of us, situations such as these trigger anger. If someone you know tells a mutual friend something negative and untrue about you, how do you feel? How do you handle it? Do you do something to annoy or hurt that person?

The self-actualized person knows that we are not separate, but that we are a part of a whole perfect system. He knows that we are always putting out an energy that demands like energy in return. He also knows that he has a choice. He can either react to the energy that is being directed at him in the same way as it comes to him, or he can choose not to be drawn into that kind of energy. When one is aware of how energy works, and is aware of his ability to choose what he wants to participate in, he can simply choose to not get involved.

Usually the ordinary person is holding so much stress in the mind/body system that he is incapable of choosing not to become involved. When we are exhausted from the demands of our life, it doesn't take much to trigger our anger. In fact, we find ourselves getting angry about things that would not bother us if we were less stressed.

The self-actualized person is seldom overstressed. He is aware of how energy works, and of the effects of an overstressed nervous system. Consequently he makes a choice to create a lifestyle that releases stress on a daily basis and keeps his nervous system strong, thereby giving him the ability to choose not to become involved in destructive energy.

Subject: Power of thought

How powerful are your thoughts? The ordinary person's mind is running constantly. He has so many thoughts going on at the same time that his thoughts are not very powerful. In fact, it is usually a challenge to keep his attention focused on one thing for very long. This is what we call our attention span. Statistics show that the attention span of the average person is quite short, and is actually decreasing. The continued and increasing stress in our lives is responsible for our inability to focus our attention.

The self-actualized person's thoughts are usually very powerful. He is capable of focusing his attention for a much longer period of time. He also has the ability to move to the project at hand regardless of what else might be going on. When our thoughts are clear and focused, they have a much greater effect on the energy field which is the source of energy for whatever we are choosing to create. Therefore, the self-actualized person has the ability to create whatever he wants in a much shorter time frame than the ordinary person.

Subject: The death of a close friend

How do you feel about death? The ordinary person is often totally overwhelmed by the death of a close friend. Again, our beliefs and the condition of our nervous systems play a major role in how we handle the death of someone close to us.

The self-actualized person sees life as eternal. The death of someone close will be a sad occasion for him, and he will certainly feel the loss. But he will see it as though his friend simply moved away to a place where he cannot see him. He will know that his friend still lives, grows and has experiences, and that the love that connected them is never destroyed or diminished.

What's the Difference?

These chapters are designed to help us see the advantages of developing our potential for self-actualization.

The self-actualized person is not a saint. He or she can make mistakes. Life's challenges are still presented, and choices must be made. The self-actualized person is simply healthier, stronger and more capable of creating the life he or she wants. The self-actualized person has tremendous advantages over the ordinary person due to the development of his intuitive abilities to understand the laws of nature. With this comes the wonderful realization that no matter what happens, he can handle it. This, I believe, is what is called peace.

What's the Difference in Relationships?

This region of truth is not to be investigated as a thing
external to us. . . . . It is within us. . . . . Consciousness,
therefore, is the sole basis of certainty. . . .
—Plotonius, third century Greek philosopher

Subject: Control

How do you get others to see things the way you do? Control
is a major issue in most relationships. The ordinary person believes that we are all separate and have minds of our own. This
makes it necessary to convince others in a relationship of the
way we see a particular situation and how we want to handle it.

The self-actualized person intuitively knows that there is
only one mind, and we are all connected in that one mind. He
also understands the law of attraction and repulsion. Therefore he knows that if he clearly knows what he wants, he will
attract others into his experience which will make it possible for
him to fulfill his desires.

The ordinary person thinks he knows the people who
should be in a particular relationship with him. Therefore he
believes that he must convince them to do what he wants. The
self-actualized person knows that he cannot make choices for
others; we all get to make our own choices. He may very well
present his case or ideas to people with whom he is now in a
relationship. However, if they choose not to participate in the
kind of relationship that he desires, he knows his desires can

still be fulfilled by being willing to accept someone else into this relationship whose desires are in harmony with his.

For example, we may be in an intimate relationship, such as marriage, with someone who does not agree with us about the major concepts of life or about how this marriage relationship should work. The ordinary person would see his only hope for having the kind of marriage he wants in somehow changing his partner's perception.

The self-actualized person would see the situation from a different perspective. Having a clearer understanding of how life works, he would have a different approach to the situation. The first step in creating anything is being very clear about what we want. The first question one might ask is: "Do I want to remain in this marriage regardless of how it affects me, or do I want to create an intimate relationship that is fulfilling for me?" Assuming the answer is the latter, which for a self-actualized person it probably would be, he would begin creating an ideal relationship for himself in his own mind. Knowing that we are all connected in the same one mind, he would know this vision creates a form in mind and starts to attract the energy necessary to fulfill it. This kind of approach is not limiting.

When we get clear about what we want to create and make a commitment to create it, a special energy emanates from us. This energy demands a like response. If our present partner can respond to that energy, he or she will probably do so. Whatever is necessary to bring this vision into our lives begins to unfold. The ordinary person would think that he must do something, such as get a divorce or start looking for another partner to bring this vision about. The self-actualized person would know that this is not at all necessary or appropriate. Whatever needs to happen simply happens. The self-actualized person would simply be open to any and all possibilities, and trust that whatever is best for all concerned will work out.

What we want in all of our relationships are like-minded people. Not people that are exactly like us, but people who want the same kind of things we do and are willing to cooperate in bringing our mutual visions to fruition.

It is important to note here that there is a law which says that we get what we expect. Or as the famous comedian, Flip Wilson, put it, "What you see is what you get." Believing something does not make it true, but it does make it our experience. If we see our partner as disagreeable, possessive, demanding or incapable, that will be our experience of him or her. It is our expectation that demands that quality to be shown to us. We act as mirrors for each other. Others will portray to us whatever we expect to see in them. Many times this is not on a conscious level. The other person may not be aware of what we see or believe about him or her, and what we believe may not even be true for him. Nevertheless, they will do whatever is necessary to help us to maintain our belief about them. Frequently, beliefs about other people are what we are projecting onto them. An example of this occurred in one of our classes in which a couple was trying to improve communications in their relationship. She complained that he didn't talk to her. She wanted him to share more with her. Things didn't seem to be changing much until one day she discovered the problem. She said, "It just occurred to me that I still believe that John will not share things with me." She changed her belief, and soon their level of communicating and sharing changed as well.

The ordinary person is totally unaware of the power of the mind and how it works with energy. The understanding of this fourth dimension which underlies all of the material world is accessed only through intuition.

Let's look at the issue of control from a different perspective. What happens if your child, even though he or she may be grown, is making choices that you totally disagree with? Do you feel a need to interfere?

The ordinary person many times feels a need to control others, especially his children. Does it work? Seldom. The self-actualized person again knows of our connection on the level of mind. Therefore he works on the level of mind. He does not see the child making the choices he thinks are appropriate; he knows that he cannot make choices for others. He simply sees the child as well and happy, not attempting to control in any

95

way the experiences that the child may need for his or her growth. In the outer realm the self-actualized parent is simply accepting and supportive. This does not mean that the parent does not express his thoughts, it simply means that he does not try to interfere by using any form of control.

The ordinary person believes that he must convince, persuade, manipulate or in some way control others. The self-actualized person knows that this is not at all necessary. He knows that he is in charge of his own life, and understands how energy works to bring people together for the benefit of all parties concerned. He knows that he attracts to himself whatever he believes in. Consequently he goes forward believing that others in his experience will be cooperative in helping him to fulfill his desires.

Subject: The need to be right

When someone disagrees with you, how important is it to you to prove to him/her that you are right? The ordinary person feels a need to be right. He believes that the information he has is correct and it is his duty to defend it. The ordinary person usually believes strongly in right and wrong. He also believes that there are very clear-cut lines between the two that everyone should be able to see.

The self-actualized person knows that right and wrong is a matter of perception. Even when we look at "the facts" they look different to different people. We could have five people read the same book and give a report on it, and the reports would be as though they had read different books. The self-actualized person knows that if we expect others to see things as we do, we will be disappointed. Our perception is determined by our own beliefs and past experiences. What could appear perfectly right to one person could seem totally wrong to another.

How much does it matter? Is it difficult for you to let others see things from a different perspective than the one you have? The ordinary person identifies with his rightness. One's ego gets involved, and sees itself as important or valuable if it considers itself to be right. Consequently, it is highly invested in proving that its perception is the correct one. Since the self-actualized person knows that right and wrong are simply different perceptions, he does not have a strong need to convince anyone else that he is right.

I have seen people get into huge arguments about almost everything they encounter together. The need to be right seems to be greater than the need to be loved. Their self-worth is connected to their ability to know what is right in any particular situation. When we have only the senses and the intellect to guide us, we are unable to understand how beliefs and perceptions work. Right and wrong are perceptions, and are therefore different for each of us. The self-actualized person understands that an absolute right or wrong does not exist, and that one person's perception is as good as another. He is guided to do what is right for him, knowing the same thing could be wrong for another. Therefore he has no need to convince anyone else that he is right. The ability to understand this could make a world of difference in people's relationships.

Subject: Blame

Do you have a tendency to blame someone else when things do not go the way you wanted? The ordinary person believes that others can and do control his life. Many times he believes that he did everything he needed to do to bring about his desired results, but someone else caused things to go wrong. He has a tendency to indulge in what we call the three deadly "C's": condemn, complain, and criticize. He has a tendency to condemn other people's perceptions and actions, complain about how they affected him, and criticize their choices.

The self-actualized person knows that he does not function as a separate entity. Given the understanding that everything in existence is energy, and that thought directs energy, the self-actualized person knows that if things do not turn out as he had planned, it is due to his lack of clarity or some other factor within himself. Consequently, he does not blame others or engage in the three deadly "C's".

Most of us have seen or been involved in relationships in which one party blamed the other for whatever went wrong for them. This produces unhealthy feelings of guilt or the need to prove one's innocence. Few relationships can withstand this kind of behavior.

The self-actualized person knows that we all create our own experiences through our own thoughts, beliefs and choices. Therefore, he takes full responsibility for his experiences, and clearly knows that if he has experiences that he does not like he can change them within himself.

Subject: The need for approval

Do you feel a need to fully impress upon others your value or importance? The ordinary person, believing that others can make or break him, finds it necessary to impress others. He wants to be sure others know how important or valuable he is. He also needs a great deal of attention and praise.

The self-actualized person feels whole and complete within himself. He knows that others' thoughts affect him very little. He may receive a lot of attention and/or praise, which he will appreciate, but he has transcended needs. He knows that it is how he feels about himself, and his own beliefs and intentions, that determine his experiences and accomplishments.

The ordinary person is motivated by his needs. He will do whatever it takes to get the attention, appreciation and approval he needs. The self-actualized person is motivated only by his inner desire to accomplish or create something of value.

Subject: Attachment

Are you attached to any of your relationships? By attachment I mean feeling that you need that person in your life in order to be complete. Again, the ordinary person sometimes thinks that he needs a certain relationship in order to be OK, and he depends on that relationship to make him a whole person.

The self-actualized person feels whole and complete within himself. He fully enjoys his relationships, but he knows that he doesn't need anyone or anything outside of himself to make him whole. He knows that indeed there is nothing outside of himself, since we are all connected and are expressions of the same source. This knowledge allows the self-actualized person to be totally free, and capable of allowing everyone to make his or her own choices.

All of our relationships are for our growth, and we do indeed grow as a result of experiencing each of them. How well our relationships work depends on the consciousness of the people involved. Remember the law of attraction and repulsion? We attract to ourselves whatever we believe in.

We are always growing toward self-actualization, and only from this level of functioning can we have truly harmonious and fulfilling relationships.

What's the Difference in Business?

*To believe your own thought, to believe that what is true
for you in your private heart is true for all men.*
—Ralph Waldo Emerson

A business organization is a reflection of the people who make up that organization. Here we want to look at how most businesses are organized and operated from the perception of the ordinary person. We also want to look at how business organizations could change as more and more people become self-actualized.

Subject: Control

Most organizations were created and designed to function around the concept of control. The organization must have a means of getting its employees to do whatever is necessary to fulfill the organization's goals.

Control is often accomplished through manipulation or intimidation. It depends on the person's perceived needs and his fear of not being able to fulfill those needs.

The ordinary person believes that he needs a job in order to make a living. The business provides a job, which pays the person the money he needs, in exchange for performance of a certain job that the company needs to have done.

Ordinary people control each other through fear. Most have a fear of losing something they believe they need. For an employee that could be the fear of losing his job. For the employer that could be the fear of losing a very valuable employee. Other needs are also used for control purposes. An example would be the person who has a need for approval. In this case a sufficient amount of attention and praise will get the job done.

When we are functioning from the use of the senses and the intellect only, we believe that we must use some form of control to get others to cooperate with us.

The self-actualized person has transcended his needs. Therefore, he cannot be manipulated, intimidated or controlled in any way. Organizations need and want the talents and abilities of self-actualized people, but they also have a resistance to them because they do not fit the organizational mold. They do not understand how the self-actualized person functions or how to get him to do what the organization wants him to do.

Subject: Motivation

The question is, "How do we motivate people?" As we have seen, the ordinary person is motivated by needs. The ordinary person has many needs (see Maslow's hierarchy of needs—Part Two, chapter 4). He also believes that others can make or break him, or, in other words, that others have control over his life.

The self-actualized person has transcended needs, or in other words, has discovered that he fulfills his own needs from within himself. The self-actualized person may want a particular job, and may do it exceptionally well, but he is motivated from within himself. He is motivated from his own inner desires, which is usually a desire to express himself or make a contribution. The self-actualized person can be enrolled in others' ideas, but only if they interest him, and he feels that they are in line with his purpose.

Subject: Integrity

How important is integrity in business? We all know that integrity is important, and that it affects trust and our ability to enroll others in our plans and goals. The ordinary person is still, however, burdened with finding a way to fulfill his needs. He also believes that what others do, say, or think will affect his ability to fulfill his needs.

The self-actualized person always does right and never does wrong (see Maslow's findings part II, chapter 4). Right and wrong, of course, is a matter of perception, and the self-actualized person's perception of right or wrong may not be the same as that of the ordinary person. What we can say is that the self-actualized person is always true to himself.

Subject: Creativity/Innovation

When we want to create something original, who is the best person for the job? What we call genius and true originality comes from the level of the superconscious. As we know, the superconscious communicates to us through intuition. The self-actualized person has developed his ability to access knowledge through intuition. Therefore, we find self-actualized people to be highly creative and innovative.

The ordinary person is limited to what he has been able to learn intellectually. He may be able to change combinations and get different results, but he doesn't have access to true originality.

Subject: Change

What happens when things are changing in an organization? The ordinary person doesn't like change. He likes to feel secure and change usually upsets his sense of security. He becomes somewhat attached to the idea of how he has done things in the past, and has a very difficult time understanding that change can be good for him and his organization.

The self-actualized person does not become attached to external circumstances. He knows that everything in the relative world is always changing, and he is quite comfortable with change. He knows himself as both changing and nonchanging. In order for change to occur there must be something stable that underlies the change. The self-actualized person knows the stable level; therefore, he knows that change is a part of the perfect order of life, and is nothing to fear.

Subject: Stability

Who can we count on? The ordinary person likes stability, and he also likes to maintain the status quo. When dramatic change occurs he often becomes overstressed and therefore less capable of maintaining his stability.

The self-actualized person knows stability from within. He knows that he is whole and complete, and nothing can change his ability to be in charge of his own life.

Subject: Flexibility

Who can go with the flow? Since the self-actualized person knows that he is in charge of his own life, external changes do not affect him as much as they might the ordinary person. Therefore, the self-actualized person can be very flexible. It is quite easy for him to change directions when he sees the need for doing so.

The ordinary person lives more by habit, and identifies more with the external world. Therefore, his ability to change course mid-stream is hampered. He does not understand that he is creating his own experiences, and this keeps him from gaining the inner stability that is necessary for change that the self-actualized person enjoys.

Subject: Longevity

How long will a person stay with an organization? The ordinary person will stay with an organization as long as his needs are being fulfilled.

The self-actualized person will stay with an organization as long as it holds his interest, and provides him with what he considers a good opportunity to express himself.

Subject: Confidence

What is the value of confidence and where do we find it? Confidence is a feeling of security, or comfort within ourselves. The self-actualized person knows himself as an expression of the source, which is whole, complete and perfect. He sees his life unfolding from within himself. Therefore, he seldom feels threatened by external circumstances.

The ordinary person may appear to be confident in the face of external confusion, but it is often an act. He does not know himself as whole and complete. He believes that others can and do control the experiences of his life.

Subject: Planning

What role does planning play in our success? The ordinary person knows he needs a plan to follow in accomplishing a specific task. He sets goals and creates a plan for accomplishing those goals.

The self-actualized person also creates plans, but he sees it from a different perspective. He first sets his goals, sees them already accomplished in his mind's eye, then he listens for intuitive guidance to guide him in designing his plan. He knows that getting clear about the goal is the most important step. When he does that he has put the creative force of intelligence and energy into action. He follows through with the plan with the realization that it can change. When he senses a need for a change he can do that without feeling any attachment to the old plan.

Subject: Leadership

How do the two differ in leadership roles? The ordinary leader has developed his ability to lead others, and in many cases does a very good job. However, he is still influenced by his own personal needs. He may also identify with his position and find it difficult to follow another's lead when that becomes necessary.

The self-actualized leader's abilities are innate, simply a part of who he is. Since he has transcended personal needs, he doesn't feel threatened by others' growth. In fact, he leads from a desire to promote growth in others. He is equally adept in following or leading. Since he does not identify with his position, he can easily follow another's lead if he agrees with the direction.

Subject: Entrepreneurial/Intrapreneurial Traits

What are these traits and where do they come from? People who possess these traits are risk-takers. They are self-starters and are willing to take full responsibility for whatever they create. Some of the traits we find in entrepreneurs are confidence, creativity, stability and flexibility. Many ordinary people are entrepreneurs. It is just a greater challenge for them than it is for the self-actualized person.

The self-actualized person has taken charge of his own life, and takes full responsibility for whatever he experiences. He possesses the traits necessary to become an entrepreneur. Whether he chooses to use his abilities in running a business or not is determined by his perception of his purpose in life.

Subject: Management Style

What determines our management style? You may be familiar with style analysis tests, which help us to become aware of how we cope with stressful situations. Our style of coping probably started when we were very young. The first thing we have to learn is how to cope with our parents. How we cope has a lot to do with what our parents rewarded. Did they think we were cute if we were entertaining, or were they looking for strict compliance, bottom line, show me what you can do? We learned how to satisfy their needs. We usually carry this style of coping with us throughout our lives unless we become conscious of our style and make a conscious effort to change it. If we can get conscious about it, we can often see that other people have other needs and expectations, and we can choose to change to better position ourselves with others.

For the ordinary person, management style is usually something we have created for ourselves over time as we grow and determine what works best. It reflects our beliefs, which may or may not have been changed over the period of our lifetime.

The self-actualized person will also have a management style, which has been created in much the same way. However, due to his ability to see things clearly and change easily, he can deal appropriately with people who have different styles. The self-actualized person has transcended needs; therefore, his style will be a reflection of a sincere desire to lead, guide and help people to become the most they can be.

Subject: Independent/Interdependent

We grow into both. The ordinary person wants to be independent—to be in charge of his own life—but is sometimes confused about how to be independent and interdependent at the same time.

The self-actualized person is independent in that he knows that he is whole and complete within himself, and is indeed in charge of the experiences in his life. He also knows that we are all connected, and that we are not separate entities; therefore, we are necessarily interdependent.

Summary

Businesses in general are designed for and run by ordinary people because there are so many more ordinary people than self-actualized people. We find few self-actualized people in business organizations because business organizations are not conducive to the free expressive life the self-actualized person chooses for himself. This forces the self-actualized person to create his own business.

Yet it is clear to see that the self-actualized person has many abilities that could greatly benefit business organizations. As more and more people become self-actualized they will create different kinds of businesses that are conducive to a free expressive life.

Life is simply easier, more enjoyable and more fulfilling for the fully developed person. Self-actualization is a natural outcome of focusing on our own personal growth.

Organizations could also greatly improve their outcomes by helping people in the organization develop their full range of abilities. Leaders for the twenty-first century and beyond will be self-actualized people. It is a human potential that we can all enjoy.

What's the Difference in Society?

All religions, arts and sciences are branches of the same tree. All these aspirations are directed toward ennobling man's life, uplifting it from the sphere of mere physical existence, leading the individual toward freedom.
—Albert Einstein

We have looked at the differences in how the ordinary person and the self-actualized person see the world and function in it. We know we are all moving toward self-actualization or maturity in our development. Many people are focusing their attention on their personal growth and are growing very rapidly. Since we are all connected, all growth affects all of us.

What kind of society will we create as more and more of us become self-actualized? How will it be different from what we see around us now?

There are people in our society today who are very immature. Their psychological abilities have not been developed to a level of awareness of cause and effect or action and consequence. They are unable to see solutions to their many problems. Their cognitive abilities are not developed; therefore, their thoughts and actions come from fear and despair. It is very easy for these people to fall into destructive thoughts and behavior. Some of these people are intellectually developed but not psychologically developed. They are not capable of fulfilling their needs, and many times make very bad choices in trying to do so.

109

On the other hand, we know that there are ordinary people living their lives from a totally different level than what we see on the evening news. These ordinary people, who make up the vast majority of our society, have reached a certain level of psychological maturity. They have discovered ways of fulfilling their needs. They are also aware of the needs of others, and to the best of their ability, they try to fulfill their needs without infringing on others.

Self-actualized people, who are the smallest percentage of our society at this time, but growing rapidly, are aware of their needs and the needs of others. They understand how all of these needs can be fulfilled from within each of us. As we have seen, they see life from a different perspective and live healthier, happier and more productive lives.

We could draw a line with one end representing the totally immature and the other representing the fully mature person. Another way to look at this line would be to label one end ignorance and the other enlightenment. We will all find ourselves somewhere between the two ends. However, we are all evolving toward full maturity, which enables us to experience enlightenment.

Most of us have heard about the new age that is taking over in the world. What does that mean? It means that we are all experiencing and observing a major paradigm shift taking place on all levels of society.

In the book *The Way Ahead,* author Robert Thurman speaks of a prophecy made in the Far East many centuries ago, which predicts that some time around now the entire planet ushers in a Golden Age. During this time individuals all over the globe find the conditions ideal for pursuing personal evolution and enlightenment. Science and technology develop unprecedented understanding and effective methods of improving the quality of life. The earth is restored and regains abundance. All beings are happy and healthy, growing intellectually and spiritually, living life meaningfully.

We believe that time is rapidly approaching. There are two waves taking place in the world today simultaneously, an upward wave and a downward wave. We see the downward wave expressed in all the crime, brutality, terrorism, and all the things that are pushing us more and more into a police state. At the same time we see the upward wave bringing us to a totally different level of existence. The downward wave consists of all that is ignorant, unintelligent, destructive and death-oriented in the world. The upward wave consists of all that is conscious, intelligent, creative and life-oriented in the world. Until recently the percentage of the population participating in the upward wave has been the minority. That's OK. Fear and destructiveness spread numerically, which is slow. Light and life-supporting creativity spread exponentially, which is fast. It is a simple law of physics. The destructive will self-destruct and the creative will become exponential in its endless power to create.

As more and more people focus their attention on self-development they will discover the fourth dimension, or spiritual dimension, of life and create a society that functions from a whole new level of understanding. Let's take a look at some of the things we might see in this new society.

Business. Today there exists a vast divide between our limited past and our boundless future. Business leaders are confused, with one foot on each side of the divide, because they lack a workable model for a knowledge-based economy.

A huge change is taking place in the business world as we see the shift from the capital centered economy of the past to the knowledge centered economy of the future. It's a new ball game with totally different rules. We need a new kind of player, one who is fully mature and capable of accessing creative ideas.

In late 1997 Bernard Ebbers, CEO of WorldCom, a small, obscure firm in Mississippi, announced that he was buying MCI. How could this former gym teacher emerge from nowhere with no capital to seize control of the second largest telecommunications company in America and gain immediate dominance over the global communications market?

It seems that one person pulled this empire together with little more than the insight of how a number of diverse companies could be integrated to deliver a complete stream of communication services around the globe. This had obviously eluded AT&T, MCI and other telecommunications giants. Because Ebbers had the intuition and vision needed to create this system, all else followed.

There are numerous other examples that show how knowledge is becoming a very powerful force in business today. Here we need to distinguish between knowledge and information. We once believed that if we only had enough information, we could do anything. We can now access more information in a split second than we could ever use. It has finally become clear that information alone is not the answer. What we need is the ability to discern what information is valuable and how it fits into the big picture. Only the self-actualized person can truly see the big picture or how all the parts fit together. The intellect is limited in its ability to comprehend the big picture. Knowledge is the knowingness of how all the parts fit together. We are now beginning to grasp the fact that knowledge, derived through intuition, is the source of all creativity and innovation. Former Shell executive Arie DeGeus says, "The critical resource now is people and the knowledge they possess."

As more and more of us become self-actualized we will be able to create businesses that function from a totally new perspective.

All organizations start from a vision. Self-actualized people come from a desire to make a contribution to the world. They are more capable of envisioning organizations that serve all concerned, since they are able to better see how we are all connected and are affected by each other.

It is likely that we will see cooperation replacing competition. The self-actualized person, knowing that we are all connected, is much more willing to share knowledge and work with others to fulfill the vision. They are also willing to share the recognition and praise.

Understanding principles of life, they are also willing to let the person or organization best qualified to perform the task do it. The self-actualized person's attitude would probably be that if someone else is better qualified than I, then they should perform the task. I will move on to where my talents are most useful. When fear is not a factor, organizations will function on a totally different level.

Government: Self-actualized people realize that there are laws of nature that govern our lives. As more and more people understand this we will have less and less need for external governing. There are unavoidable consequences for making choices that are not in harmony with the laws of nature. The self-actualized person is aware of these laws and makes choices accordingly.

Real power comes from within, and we will begin to realize that external forces cannot regulate people's behavior. People change their behavior only when they have an understanding of why it needs to change. Crime will naturally disappear as more and more people become aware of the principles of life and how they work.

Government is based on a belief in external control. As people become aware of the power we each have within ourselves, government as we have known it in the past will no longer be appropriate.

War: The self-actualized person has no need for war. Since everything is energy, and we direct and form this energy through our thoughts, beliefs and expectations, we can create whatever we want. Resources are unlimited. We create our own boundaries; they are not created by others. The self-actualized person knows that the source of all of creation is Love, and we are all expressions of this Love, Intelligence and Energy. There is also a clear realization that Love is all powerful.

Traffic accidents: Would a self-actualized person drive irresponsibly? Would he drive with his senses impaired? It looks as if we can also look forward to fewer traffic accidents.

Relationships: The closer to full maturity we become the better our relationships will be. When we are not aware of our own wholeness, we attract people to us to mirror our misunderstandings back to us. This is perfect for our growth, but does not produce relationships that are as good as they could be if both parties knew their own wholeness. When we feel whole and complete within ourselves we no longer need others to do or say specific things to make us feel good about ourselves. When we are no longer needy it is easy to allow others to be who they are, and appreciate our differences as well as our similarities. As more and more of us become self-actualized, relationships will become more harmonious and fulfilling.

Families: Self-actualized people know themselves as expressions of Love. Love is the foundation for a family. They are aware that each individual gets to make his own choices, and according to the laws of nature, will experience the consequence of these choices. The self-actualized parent doesn't operate out of fear; therefore, fear is not passed on to the children.

Summary

Self-actualized people are simply ordinary people who have grown in maturity. They are healthier, happier and more capable of creating the lives they want for themselves. They have the ability to access knowledge from a source not available to others; therefore, they see the world from a different perspective.

At this point in time we can just begin to comprehend some of the changes that will take place in our society as more and more of us move into this realm of functioning. The world we have known in the past will change dramatically on all fronts.

I hope that this quick glance at how things could change for each of us has convinced you that self-actualized is the only way to be. Moving to this new level of functioning requires time and commitment, but I hope you can see that it is well worth the effort.

In Part Four a process is provided for you to follow to reach this level of maturity. Many people have followed this process with remarkable results. As we all realize our oneness, we can create the lives we want for ourselves, and together we can create a whole new world for all of us.

Part Four

From Caterpillars to Butterflies

A New Lifestyle—A New Life

Truth is not introduced into the individual from without, but within him all the time.—Sören Kierkegaard, nineteenth century Danish philosopher

It is now time to begin spinning our cocoons, creating a place that makes it possible for us to experience our own metamorphosis. It is now time to create a lifestyle that will allow us to experience self-actualization.

The first step is commitment. Consider W. H. Murray's statement: "Until one is committed there is hesitancy, the chance to draw back, always ineffectiveness. Concerning all acts of initiative (and creation), there is one elementary truth, the ignorance of which kills countless ideas and splendid plans: the moment one definitely commits oneself, then providence moves, too. All sorts of things occur to help that would never otherwise have occurred. A whole stream of events issues from the decisions, raising in one's favor all manner of unforeseen incidents, meetings and material assistance, which no man could have dreamt would have come his way."

All accomplishments require commitment. I hope by now you are ready to make a full commitment to creating a lifestyle that will lead you to higher and higher levels of personal growth and self-actualization. Creating this new lifestyle is the most important thing you have to do if you want to create this new way of functioning.

117

There is a routine of things that you need to do on a daily basis in order to refine the energy in the mind/body system so that it is capable of merging with the more refined energy of the superconscious.

We know that everything is made up of energy, and energy vibrates from low levels of density—a rock, for example—to higher levels of refinement which we find in the human. However, the ordinary person's energy is not sufficiently refined to allow him to intuitively know himself.

The stress in our lives blocks our ability to know who we are on a higher level. In order to release the stress stored in the mind/body system and refine the energy which makes up the system, we must make a commitment to a daily routine of breathing exercises, stretching exercises and meditation.

When we schedule these practices into our daily lives, our lives begin to change; however, you may or may not feel the subtle changes in the energy in your mind and body. Either way, the energy will begin to change and you will begin to feel peaceful and calm inside. The mind will stop racing constantly and thoughts will become clearer. Your ability to focus your attention will increase.

These are subtle changes that have accumulative effects over time. Please do not expect fireworks; this is an inner process, not an outer one.

It is also highly recommended that you eliminate as much stress as possible from your life. Many things cause stress in our lives, the major one being our own thoughts and beliefs, which we will work with later. For now, start to observe how you feel when you are in the company of different people. Try to associate with people who bring a positive energy and with whom you feel good. You will discover that you feel uplifted after being in the presence of some people, and drained of your energy after being with others. Also notice how you are affected by entertainment. Some entertainment will leave you feeling uplifted, while some others will leave you drained.

One of the most powerful tools we have to use for our growth is observation. As we observe how we relate to the energy around us, our consciousness expands and we are able to make better choices. Remember that you are in charge and you get to make all of your own choices and experience all the consequences.

Let's get started now with the breathing and stretching exercises that start to refine the mind/body energy. First choose a place where you can be alone and not be disturbed while doing your routine. It is beneficial to have a special blanket that you use just for exercise.

It is recommended that you start your day with this process. Repeating the process in the early evening is also recommended if you want to grow as fast as possible. The process should be done in the morning before breakfast and the evening before dinner. It should be done on an empty stomach. If you choose to do the exercises in the late evening, wait at least three hours after eating.

We have named these stretching exercises "energizers" to help you understand that they have a totally different purpose than aerobics, running, or calisthenics. These energizers activate the energy centers in the body that lie dormant if not activated. This activation not only gives more energy, it also allows the stress stored in the body to be released. It allows the body to become settled, thereby allowing the mind to also become settled and calm. This brings the entire system to a state of deep rest. It is the nature of the system, given sufficient rest, to heal itself and strengthen itself. Each of the energizers has a physically healing and strengthening effect on specific areas of the body. Doing all of the energizers in the following order provides healing, strengthening and revitalizing for the entire physiology.

These are relaxing exercises and need to be performed slowly and smoothly. *Never force or strain.* You want to allow your body to relax into the posture. Another thing that is important to understand in doing the energizers is that this process includes both the mind and the body. Consequently, we need to keep our attention focused on the body while doing the exercises. You want to be totally with the body, to experience how it feels as it moves. Bring your attention to whatever area of the body you are working with, and become fully aware of that area of your body. This begins to expand our awareness of the interrelatedness of the mind and body, and begins to develop the mind's ability to focus.

We start the process in the morning with three purifying breaths. Go outside, or at least get your head outside, and take a deep breath, inhaling through the nose. Then exhale forcefully through the mouth, exhaling all the stale air that has settled in the lungs overnight. Do this three times, no more. It is helpful to use the arms and hands as though you are pulling the air in and throwing it out.

Now come inside, spread your blanket and let's get started. Sit in the middle of your blanket in a comfortable crossed-leg position. We want to start this process with a breathing exercise. First you want to notice your usual way of breathing, and how deep breaths and shallow breaths affect your energy. Place your hand on your abdomen, and inhale deeply, as though you are bringing the air all the way down into the abdomen. Your abdomen should expand as you breathe in. Now, exhale, releasing all the air, pulling in the abdomen. Notice how you feel as you continue to take these deep breaths. This is the way we should always breathe. This gives you maximum use of the oxygen in the air, and also creates a relaxed, peaceful feeling. Just for comparison, let's also try a shallow breath. Place your hand on the upper part of your chest. Now breathe into the chest only. Notice how the shallow breath makes you feel. The breath automatically becomes shallow when we feel anxious.

You will want to notice how you are breathing periodically throughout the day. If you find your breath is shallow and short, consciously change it to the long deep breaths as described above. The breath is the link between the mind and body, and this form of breathing on a regular basis will begin to bring the mind and body into synchronicity.

To prepare the body for our stretching exercises, we will do a self-massage (see next page). Begin by taking the palms of your hands and press gently on your forehead, over your eyes, down the face and neck to your heart. Now clasp your hands

#1. Self-Massage

together and start, by applying pressure to the back of your head, then move the hands apart and massage over the shoulders, then back to the heart.

Now hold one arm out as if you are going to shake hands with someone. Then take the other hand and start massaging the hand and arm, up the top side of the arm, and down to the heart. Then massage the hand and arm up the bottom side and down to the heart. Do the same thing with the other hand and arm. Next take one foot into both of your hands and massage the foot and up the leg with one hand on each side of the leg, then bring one hand up the front of the body and one up the back to the heart. Repeat with the other leg.

Next we go to #2 (below), the Body Roll. Lie flat on your back, bend your knees and, bringing them to your chest, clasp your hands together over your legs. Now roll to your right, keeping your head on the floor. Bring your head all the way around so that you are looking back the other way. Now roll to the left the same way. Perform this exercise ten times, five each way.

#2. The Body Roll

After the rolls, go into #3 (below), the Bicycle, using your legs as you would pedal a bicycle, for about ten to twenty times. Then stretch the body out. After a good stretch, bring your arms down to your side, palms up, and totally relax. Remain in this relaxed position for about three minutes.

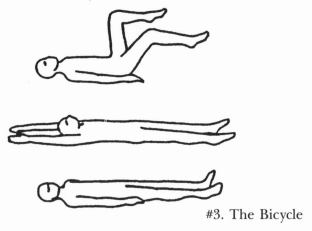

#3. The Bicycle

Now we move to #4 (below), the Toner. Stand on your knees with your hands clasped together, palms up, in front of you. Push your arms and hands down, while tightening the buttocks and leaning backward. Hold this position for a count of ten.

#4. The Toner

Next we go to #5 (next page), the Back Arch. Place your hands on the floor behind you as you sit back on your heels, then lift your body up off the legs. Remember, never strain. Perform each exercise only to the degree that it is slightly stretching for you. As you continue to do the exercises daily you will

#5. The Back Arch

become more limber, and it will get easier and easier. As you proceed you are getting exactly what you need if you are stretching, but not hurting yourself. If for any reason you should hurt yourself, even slightly, discontinue that exercise until your body has healed itself.

Now to #6 (below), the Camel. Bring the body up straight on your knees, then lean back, bringing your hands to your ankles to support you. Remember you do not have to do it perfectly the first time. Let your body limber up at its own speed.

#6. The Camel

Now to #7 (next page), Limbering the Legs and the Lotus Position. Start this posture by sitting in a comfortable crossed-leg position. Take one leg by the ankle and bring the other arm around the knee, as if you are holding a baby, then rock the leg back and forth, just limbering it up, about five times. Then repeat the same procedure with the other leg. Usually after many months of the limbering procedure you can begin to place one foot on the top of the opposite leg, then bring the other leg over the top of that leg, and tuck your foot behind the knee. Please do not try to force this in any way. It took me three years to be able to sit in this position. Yet my husband could do it

#7. Limbering the Legs and the Lotus Position

right away. How well we can do each of the postures varies with how we are built. Please be observant and respectful of your body. Once you master this position, it becomes very comfortable, and holds your back straight for other postures.

Until you are comfortable with the lotus position, just sit in a comfortable cross-legged position and move into #8 (below), the Neck Roll.

#8. The Neck Roll

This keeps the neck limber and releases the stress stored there. Let your chin fall toward your chest, and slowly roll your head all the way around. Do this three times in each direction.

After the neck roll, move to #9 (below), Drop Ear Toward Shoulder.

Bring the head straight up, then bring your right ear down toward your right shoulder. Hold for a couple of seconds, then repeat on the left side.

#9. Drop Ear Toward Shoulder

No. 10 (below), the Chin-Eye Exercise, is performed by jutting the chin out and turning the head as far as possible to the right, and at the same time stretching the eyes to the right to look as far as possible behind you. This is a great eye exercise for peripheral vision and it also allows light to stimulate the pituitary gland.

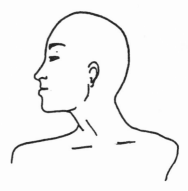

#10. The Chin-Eye Exercise

Now to #11 (next page), the Forward Bend. At first this will be done from a crossed-leg position, but after you are comfortable with the lotus position start in that position. Bring your arms out straight in front of you, turn the hands over so the palms are facing outward, then bring the arms behind your back and clasp your hands together. Pull the arms up as high as you can while bending forward toward the floor in front of you. Hold this position for about ten seconds.

#11. The Forward Bend

Next we move to #12, the Backward Bend. Still in this crossed-leg position, or lotus, bring your arms behind you, holding your waist with your hands in back and rest your weight on your elbows and lower arms, then let your head fall backward. Hold this position for about ten seconds. This should be a very comfortable, easy, stretch.

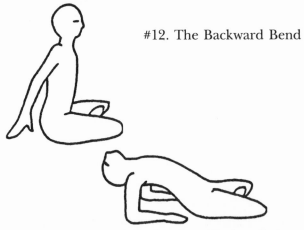

#12. The Backward Bend

Next comes #13 (next page), the Arm Circles. Sit in a comfortable crossed-leg position, hold your arms out straight, then make as large a circle as possible with each arm, bringing your arms up as high as you can, and down just skimming the floor.

Circle arms in a forward motion for ten times, then reverse and circle in the opposite direction.

#13. Arm Circles

Now to #14, Upper Arm Tension. Bring your hands together in front of you, push the palms together until you feel the muscles in the upper arm strengthening. Now rotate hands back and forth, then push hands and arms from one side to the other.

#14. Upper Arm Tension

Now we move to #15 (next page), Stretch Over Knee. In a sitting position, bring one leg straight out in front of you. Bend the other knee and place the sole of the foot against the inside of your leg as close to the crotch as possible. Now hold the outstretched leg with your hands and bring your body forward, bringing the head toward the knee. Again, do not strain. If you can only bow your head to begin with, that is a start. As you continue with the energizers it becomes easier and easier to simply flow into the positions. Hold this position for a count of ten to twenty. Start with a count of ten and build up to a count of twenty. Now repeat this posture with the other leg.

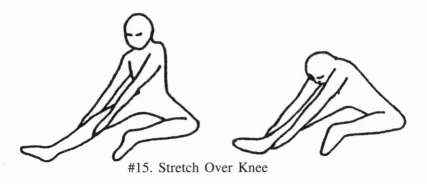

#15. Stretch Over Knee

Next we go to #16 (below), the Plow with Shoulder Stand. If you have a back problem of any kind, please check with your physician before doing this exercise. This exercise begins from a sitting position, with legs straight out in front of your body. Grasp the legs with each hand at any place that works for you, then bring your head down toward your knees. Then bend your knees and roll backward, bringing your legs up over your head. Bring your arms to the floor and support your back with both hands on your waist. Now tuck your chin into the hollow space just below your neck and bring your legs up as straight as possible. Hold this position for a count of ten, building to twenty. To come out of this position, bend your knees and roll out smoothly. You can clasp your arms around your knees if that helps. Roll back into a sitting position, then repeat the exercise one more time.

#16. Plow with Shoulder Stand

This brings us to #17 (below), Feet Together, Knees to Floor. Bring the soles of your feet together. Hold your feet together with your hands and bring your knees toward the floor.

#17. Feet Together, Knees to Floor

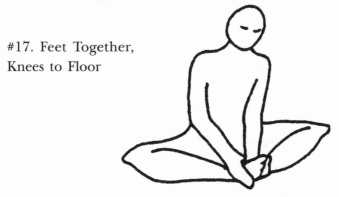

Next is #18, Straddle Leg Splits. Stretch your legs in front of you as far as is comfortable. Place one hand on each leg and bring your head toward the floor between your legs. Again, be easy with yourself. I have seen people who could only bow their heads and others who were very limber and easily could put their heads to the floor. Again, you only want to do what is simply stretching for you.

#18. Straddle Leg Splits

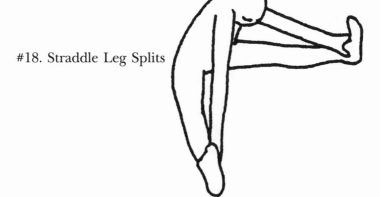

Number 19 (next page), Total Relaxation, is just what we need now. The next few exercises will be done from a horizontal position on the floor, and you should rest between each of them. How long you rest depends on how much time you have allotted, but please do not skip the rests. The rest periods are just as important as the exercises. The idea is to stretch the body, then totally relax it. For the total relaxation, lie flat on the floor on your stomach, arms down by the side, palms up. This is also an exercise for the neck. Lie the face flat on the floor on one side, then on the other, looking to the left after one exercise and the right after the next. This first relaxation should last at least three minutes. You can count or determine the time by feel.

#19. Total Relaxation

Then on to #20, the Cobra. Bring your head straight up from the floor, now bend your elbows and bring your hands together, fingers facing each other, in front of your face. Now push backward, lifting your chest off the floor, but not the stomach. Now keeping the elbows bent turn your neck and eyes to where you can see the heel of the opposite foot on one side; then turn your head in the other direction and check the other foot. When you first start the exercises you might need to raise

#20. The Cobra

your foot off the floor a little to help get it in your range of sight. Now rest and then repeat the cobra exercise once more.

Next we move to #21 (below), the Body Rock. From the rest position, bend one knee and bring the leg up to where you can grasp the ankle with the hand. Now do the same thing on the other side, making a rocker of your body. Lift the head and chest and the legs off the floor and rock back and forth. This may be a bit of a challenge at first; do whatever works for you.

#21. The Body Rock

Please do not strain or hurt yourself. As you continue to work with the postures, your body will limber up, but never force your body into a position. Just keep moving your body in that direction, and one day it will go into the position easily. Once you are in this position, hold it for a count of ten, then begin the rock. Rock back and forth five times, building up to ten over time. Now relax again.

Once the body feels totally relaxed again, move on to #22 (below), the Leg Lift. Still lying on your stomach, bring your arms down by your side, hold each arm straight and make two fists. Press down on your fists and arms while lifting your legs up from the floor without bending your knees. Hold this position for a count of ten, building to twenty. Rest, then repeat the leg lift once more.

#22. The Leg Lift

From your rest position move on to #23 (below), the Cat Stretch. Bring your hands up in front of you, then push your body up, stretching the back. Now keeping your hands flat on the floor, stretch backward to where you are sitting on your lower legs and ankles with the head and body stretched out in front of you.

#23. The Cat Stretch

Now from this position go into #24 (below), the Balance. Balance your weight on your right knee and your left hand, then bring your left leg and your right arm up to a balanced position. Keep your sight on the right hand that is up in front

#24. The Balance

of you. Hold this position for a count of ten, building to twenty. Now repeat on the other side. Balance your weight on the left knee and the right hand, bringing the right leg and the left arm up, keeping your eyes on the left hand. Now rest again.

#25. The Cat Stretch

Now move on to #25, which is just a repeat of the cat stretch one more time. After this, move into a sitting position.

This brings us to #26 (below), the Twist. Starting from a sitting position, bring the right leg straight out in front of you. Now bend the knee of the left leg and place the left foot flat on the floor on the opposite side of the right leg, parallel with the right knee. Now put your left arm behind you. Bring your right arm behind the other side of the left knee and hold onto the left ankle. Now twist your body to the left looking as far behind you as possible; hold for a count of five, then turn the head to look over your right shoulder, and hold for a count of five. Now repeat the entire procedure on the other side, bringing your left leg out straight and bringing your right foot on the

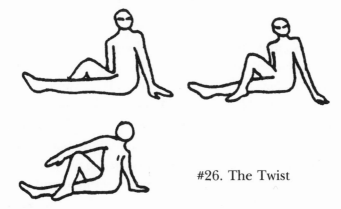

#26. The Twist

outer side of the left knee. Put the right hand behind you and bring your left arm around the outside of your right leg and twist your body and head to look over your left shoulder; hold for a count of five, then back to look over your right shoulder for a count of five. This will definitely take some concentration for beginners, but once you get it right you will experience a very nice stretch. Now, repeat the whole procedure once more. This posture can also be done with the leg that starts out straight being bent so that the foot is touching the thigh of the other leg before it is brought over the opposite knee.

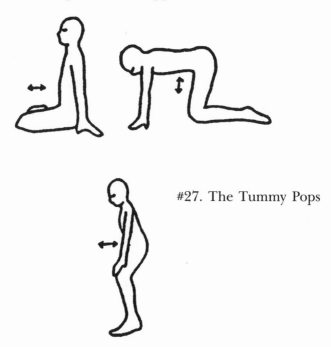

#27. The Tummy Pops

Next we move to #27 (above), the Tummy Pops. If you are not a belly dancer, we are going to focus on some muscles that you probably haven't focused on for a while. We will start this one from a crossed-leg sitting position. Take a deep, full breath and bring the air all the way down into the stomach. Remember that this is how we want to be breathing all the time now. Then exhale. After exhaling and before inhaling again, pull the stomach muscles in and up, then try popping them in and out a few times before inhaling again. Be easy with it. At the beginning just go with the timing you feel is right for your breathing. After a while, do ten pops in and out, building to twenty in each of the positions. Next move to where you are standing on your hands and knees. Now repeat the full breath, and after exhaling pull your stomach in and up, and pop it in and out. Next move to a standing position. Place your feet apart, about level with your shoulders; bend your knees and place your hands on your knees, fingers facing inward. Now repeat the full breath, and after you exhale bring your stomach in and up, then pop it in and out several times before inhaling again.

This brings us to #28 (below), Touch the Toes. Bring the body straight up, raise the arms over the head and stretch upward as far as possible. Now relax and bend forward to whatever level is comfortable for you. In time you will probably be able to touch the floor.

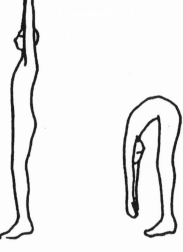

#28. Touch the Toes

This brings us to #29 (below), Total Relaxation. This time we relax on the back. Lie down flat on your back, arms down by your sides with your palms facing up, close your eyes, and let your body totally relax. Rest three to five minutes.

#29. Total Relaxation

Now to #30 (below), the Bridge. After your rest, bend your knees, place your feet flat on the floor and bring them up as close to the buttocks as possible. Then, bring your arms up over your shoulders, elbows bent, fingers pointing toward your feet. Then try raising your body up off the floor, putting your weight on your hands and feet. Hold for a count of ten, building to a count of sixty. This one will also probably take some time for many people. If you can't raise your body off the floor, just lift the buttocks up, resting your weight on your feet and shoulders. Continue to work with it without strain; whatever you can do is perfect for you at the time. Rest after this posture.

#30. The Bridge

Then go to #31 (next page), the Modified Headstand. From a position on your knees, clasp your hands together, bend your elbows, and put your hands and arms on the floor in front of you, making a cradle for your head. Now place the top of your forehead on the floor just behind your hands. Lift your buttocks into the air, putting your weight on your arms and head. For beginners, come down as soon as you feel the need. As you continue with this posture, hold it for a count of thirty, building to a count of one hundred and twenty. When you are ready to come down, simply bend your knees, and roll over onto your back without taking your head off the floor.

#31. Modified Headstand

This brings us back to #32 (below), Total Relaxation. Relax for at least a couple of minutes before getting up.

#32. Total Relaxation

This concludes the postures, or what we like to call energizers. This set of energizers works on all areas of the body to release stress, strengthen the nervous system and refine the mind/body energy, thereby preparing one for higher and higher levels of health and wellness. These energizers are a part of the preparation of the mind/body energy which allows us to tap into our intuitive abilities.

Sometimes people tell me they simply do not have time to do all of these exercises. It is not about time, it is about beliefs and choices. They find that when they make a choice to do this process, they seem to actually have more time. It is a process that allows you to do less and accomplish more in the same time frame. When you are functioning better, it actually takes less time to accomplish the same tasks.

After doing the exercise routine, your body is prepared for the next step—another breathing exercise then meditation, which will be described in the next chapter.

16 Meditation

*In silence, a being is identified with its pure freedom, with
that pure possibility of itself, which it discovers when it
retires within itself.*—Gisele Brelet,
twentieth century French writer

The next step in developing our ability to create the life we want
for ourselves is training our conscious awareness to connect
with who we are on a deeper level. Another way to say that is to
learn how to merge our conscious mind with the
superconscious. This is accomplished through meditation. As
an example, imagine a circle with a dot in the center. Let the
circle represent the ordinary mind, which is busily thinking
thoughts constantly, or, in other words, going around and
around the circumference of the circle. If we can teach the mind
to slow down and stay focused on one point, it begins to move
toward the center of the circle, which represents the
superconscious, the source of all intelligence and energy. When
we merge the conscious mind with the superconscious on a
regular basis, the conscious mind begins to expand, and we
begin to experience a knowingness about the laws of nature
and how we create our own experiences.

There are a number of ways to meditate, and I will describe
several for you to choose from. I recommend that you try all of
them, then choose the one that works best for you. We will
begin with short forms of meditation, but once we become adept

at it we will meditate for twenty minutes twice a day, after doing each set of our energizers once in the morning before breakfast and then in the evening before dinner. The exercises prepare the body to settle down for meditation.

Before we begin our meditation, we want to do another breathing exercise. This is called the balanced breath. This breathing exercise balances the energy in our bodies, allowing the entire mind/body system to relax and settle down in preparation for meditation (see drawing below).

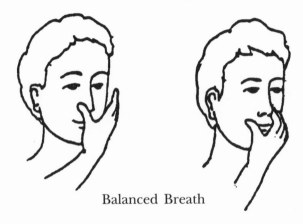

Balanced Breath

Use your right hand if you are male, and your left hand if you are female. Close off one side of your nostrils with your thumb, and breathe in through the other side. Now release that side and close off the other nostril with your second finger and your ring finger and exhale through the other side. Now inhale through the same side, close the nostril on the other side with your thumb again, and exhale. Continue this process for two minutes once you have mastered it. For beginners, do whatever feels comfortable for you.

The purpose of meditation is to bring the conscious mind to the level of the superconscious, or, in other words, to transcend the intellect, to go beyond the intellect (thinking process) and merge with the source of everything, which we find at the level of pure silence. We can use any of the senses to help us reach this level of silence. The idea is to focus our attention on one point. Start by simply focusing your attention on your breath.

Sit comfortably in a chair or in a crossed-leg position with something supporting your back. The idea is to be very comfortable, so as not to be distracted by your body. Place your hands in your lap, close your eyes and begin to focus your attention on your breathing. Breathe comfortably, as you usually breathe. Notice the breath as it comes in, bring it all the way down into your abdomen, then slowly exhale, keeping your attention on your breath all the time. If thoughts slip in, as soon as you are aware of them simply bring your attention back to your breath. Continue this process for three to five minutes. You can notice the clock before you start, then again afterwards. You will soon be able to feel the right timing. Do not set an alarm of any kind to measure your meditation time. The entire system will become very settled and any kind of alarm will jar the system, which causes stress. When the time is up, slowly open your eyes and come back to outer consciousness. Then remain sitting for a couple of minutes before returning to your activities.

After using the above technique for a week, let's work with another meditation technique using the sense of sight. Select an object that you enjoy looking at; it could be a vase, a figurine, or anything else that pleases you, and place it about three feet in front of you. Sit in a comfortable position, and focus your attention on the object. Try to simply be with the object for about three minutes. The idea is not to think about the object, but to simply observe it. Notice how often your mind wanders onto other things. Don't be distracted by these thoughts, and don't try to force them out. Simply bring your attention back to the object when you discover that you are off onto other thoughts. Observe how this technique works for you.

Next let's try candle concentration. Prepare for meditation in the usual way. Then place a candle in a holder that will catch the melting wax, and light it. Place it about three feet in front of you, on the same level at which you are sitting. Now look at the flame of the candle and keep your focus on the flame for about two minutes. Again, when the mind wanders simply bring it back to the flame. After a couple of minutes of focusing on the flame of the candle, close your eyes and bring the palms of your hands up to cover your eyes. Now look for the flame with your eyes closed. You will most likely detect the flame in some form. Just be with it. If you lose it, just bring it back by continuing to look for it. Practice this for another two minutes. Now reflect on your experience.

Observation is a very important tool in discovering who we are and how life works.

Be very gentle with yourself in all of the meditations. Never try to force anything, and do not get caught up in an argument with yourself. You have all the power. Even though old habits do not die easily, simply bring your attention to where you want it to be, and continue to do this as many times as is necessary. The ordinary mind is accustomed to having its way, and will resist being disciplined, but in time it will learn.

Another technique you can use with the sense of sight is to simply bring your attention to focus on anything in your surroundings. It could be a spot on the floor or wall. You can do this at any time, like when you are waiting in an office or waiting for an elevator. What we are doing now is teaching the mind to be able to focus. As we move into creating the things we want in our lives, you will see the value of this. It is the strength of our thoughts and the clarity of our thoughts that determine the speed of our manifestations.

Next let's use the sense of sound for focusing our attention. Select a recording of some music that you particularly like. It needs to be music only, no words, and something that makes you feel good, not excited. After finishing your energizers and the breathing exercises, lie comfortably on your blanket or sit in a comfortable chair and play your music for about five minutes. Do not think about the music; simply experience it. Let yourself be an instrument through which the music plays. If you have thoughts that come in, just bring your attention back to the music and continue to be with it. Gently let the thoughts go whenever they arise.

For most people, using the sense of sound seems to be the most effective form of meditation, since the idea is to bring the conscious mind to the level of silence. I was using the next technique when I had my first experience of profound knowingness and understanding of the laws of nature and how they work.

Again, prepare for meditation as usual; sit comfortably with your spine straight, arms and hands in a comfortable position. Close your eyes, completely relax, and listen for a sound that is within yourself. The mystics say this is the sound of creation being created. Different people describe it differently. I do not know if we hear different sounds or if we just describe them differently. To me it is a humming sound, although some describe it like the sound you hear from a seashell, and still others describe it as a ringing sound. Whatever you hear is fine. Most of the time when we start listening, we hear outside sounds first, but if we just keep listening we will connect with this inner sound. Once we connect with it, it can become quite loud. This inner sound is much closer to the source than outer sounds, and once we connect with it, it is easy to transcend the sound and merge with pure silence. Even the slightest experience of pure silence brings great benefits.

Each time we meditate we merge with the silence, the source of all sound, energy and intelligence. These experiences have an accumulative effect. This is why we need to meditate twice a day, every day. Each time we merge our conscious mind with the superconscious we return with an expanded awareness. Over time we find that we automatically make better choices, and we begin to understand how the creative process works through the laws of nature. Changes start to take place in our lives; many times we cannot explain it, but we simply know what to do and how to do it. Meditating on a regular basis is how we develop our intuition. The longer we work with the process the more we experience that knowingness until it is a part of our everyday lives, and we can hardly even remember what it was like not knowing.

All the techniques for meditation are simply tools for training the conscious mind to merge with the superconscious. Our goal is to merge with the silence. We use the tools or meditation techniques that work best for us to reach that goal.

Next we will discuss mantra meditation. A mantra is simply a word or thought to use for focusing our attention on one point, preparing us for our journey inward. There are many mantras or sounds that we can use. Sometimes someone will ask me, "Why can't I just pick a word, and use it as a mantra?" Because the sound of the word we use as a mantra is very important, since a sound of a word and the meaning of the word are interrelated. Different sounds have different effects in the energy fields. The Transcendental Meditation movement has made mantra meditation popular. There have been numerous scientific studies done on transcendental meditation, and the findings have shown outstanding benefits for its practitioners. A TM teacher initiates a person into the practice of meditation and gives him/her a mantra that is selected for that person from some specific criteria. These mantras are supposed to be a sound only. At least you do not know the meaning of the sound. This sometimes makes it easier to transcend our numerous thoughts than when we use a mantra that has a meaning. You can find transcendental meditation centers in most major cities. I used TM for many years and found it very valuable. In addition to teaching meditation, the movement also provides other growth opportunities.

The mantra "OM" is used frequently. This is supposed to be the sound of creation being created. I have found that using this mantra in a group, where each participant takes a deep breath and uses half the breath to make the sound "O", then the remaining breath to make the sound "M", all in unison, is a very powerful experience. If you would like to experience it, sit with your back straight, just as in all meditations, take a full deep breath, then make the sound "O" as you exhale half the breath, then sound the letter "M" with the remaining breath. Do this seven times, then sit quietly and notice if you can feel the vibration of the energy around you. It can also be used as an internal sound if it is not appropriate to use it out loud. The experience will be different, but still powerful. As we know, the more subtle the vibration the more powerful it is. We just are not as consciously aware of it.

The mantra we have selected to use is the word "Love." Since the sound of a word and the meaning of the word are closely related, "Love" is most appropriate. We use the word "Love" to describe the source of creation and the source of all power. We use the mantra to bring the conscious mind to one point to begin its journey to the superconscious, found on the level of absolute silence. When using "Love" as a mantra we are not at all concerned with the meaning of the word, we are using it for the quality of the vibration of the word. We do not want to get caught up in thinking about the meaning of the word. We simply repeat it over and over, and the vibration of this thought brings the conscious mind toward its source.

Now let's try it. After the energizers, and the balanced breath, sit comfortably with your back straight. Put your hands in your lap, close your eyes, let yourself settle down, then start thinking the word "Love." Think the word "Love" over and over in an easy manner, just as you would think any other thought. When you notice that your mind has wandered off onto another thought, simply bring it back to the mantra. As you repeat the mantra it may speed up or slow down; that doesn't matter. Just keep your mind focused on this one word or sound. After awhile the mind will tire of this sound and will automatically transcend it, and merge with the superconscious on the level of pure silence. This is the purpose of all meditation.

We recommend that you meditate for twenty minutes twice a day. You might want to start with a ten-minute meditation, but soon you will not want to come out of meditation in ten minutes. In whatever way is comfortable for you, increase your meditation to twenty minutes. Set a clock where you can see it. Notice the time when you start your meditation, then when it feels like the time is up, simply open your eyes and check the clock. If the time is not up, just close your eyes and continue meditating. Once again, do not set an alarm when you are meditating. An alarm will jolt the nervous system and create stress.

If you should fall asleep during your meditation, it just means that you need more sleep; therefore, your system is not capable of maintaining awareness at that time. When you wake

145

up and realize that you have been sleeping, simply go back to your meditation. If your allotted time is up, it is still good to go back into meditation for a few minutes. After meditation, let go of the mantra, sit quietly with your eyes closed for a couple of minutes, then slowly open your eyes and take a few minutes to bring your attention back to outer consciousness before moving.

Remember that meditation is about letting go of thoughts and bringing the conscious mind back to silence, its source. Choose the technique that works best for you, but set aside twenty minutes for meditation twice a day. The first thing in the morning is the best time for our full routine of breathing exercises, stretching exercises and meditation. This prepares you to be at your best throughout the day. If you put this into your schedule every morning you will notice a great difference in how your day goes. Late in the afternoon before dinner is another perfect time to do the full routine again.

Every time you do the stretching exercises, the breathing exercises and meditation, you release the stress that has accumulated in your body, and refine the mind/body energy, which enables you to intuitively know the laws of nature and how to make choices in harmony with these laws to create the life you want. When we do not have a program for releasing the stress on a daily basis, we simply go around and around the circumference of the circle, functioning in the same old limiting ways, and creating the same old things, and never understanding why things happen as they do.

This process practiced on a daily basis will lead you to a whole new way of life. It will create better health, broaden your horizons, allow you to see many more possibilities and enhance your ability to live a life of peace, joy and happiness.

Before concluding this chapter I want to give you one more stretching exercise. This one exercise allows the body to relax with just one routine of stretches. If you simply cannot do your full set of exercises one evening, then you can substitute this routine to prepare yourself for meditation. This routine can also be used as an aerobic exercise in the morning. If you are

146

using the routine to prepare for meditation when you cannot do the full set of exercises, follow the chart through the fourteenth position, then go back to #4 and go through the whole routine again, starting with the left leg instead of the right this time. Follow the routine all the way through.

If you would like to use this routine as an aerobic exercise you may do the routine six times, three times on each side. Start with #1 (below), being observant of your posture before starting. Follow through to #14, then return to #4, and use your left foot instead of the right for the next set. Continue this, alternating the starting leg each time. After six sets, complete the routine with postures #15 through #19. When using this routine with your full set of postures, it fits in after you have finished the bicycle and rested. It comes before exercise #4.

Start this routine in a standing position with palms of hands together in front of you, as seen in the diagram. Be sure you are standing straight and your posture is just the way you want it to be. After observing your posture, bring your arms up over your head, clasp hands together, palms facing up, then stretch as far as you can without pain to one side, then the other. Now bring arms up over your head, palms facing out, stretch back a little, and inhale deeply. Now bring your hands down to the floor, supporting your weight on your hands and feet, making an upside-down **V**-position with your body, and exhale. Next bring your right leg up, knee bent into a running pose, look up and inhale. Now bring your feet back together, body in the upside-down **V**-position again and exhale. Now bend the knees and lower your body to the floor. Bend elbows and place hands, fingers facing in, under your head, and push back, keeping stomach on the floor, and inhale. Next push yourself up into the inverted **V**-position again and exhale. Now bring your left foot forward, knee bent into a runner's start pose, look up and inhale. Now bring your foot back, putting your body into the inverted **V**-position, and exhale. Now bring your body straight up, inhale and start over with the same procedure, this time alternating legs, starting with the left leg instead of the right one. Do the routine as many times as you choose, then finish

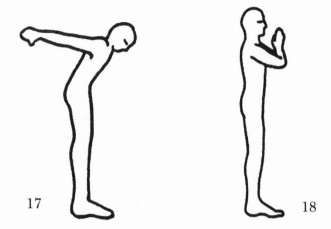

17   18

the routine by bringing the hands, palms together, in front of you, while standing with a straight, perfect posture. Now extend your arms out, palms outward, clasp hands together behind you and bend backward as far as you can, breathing in. Then bend over to the front as far as possible, bringing your arms up behind you as far as you can, and exhale. Then finish with the salutation position.

This is also a good exercise for concentration on the breath. Remember, you breathe in when the head is up and out when it is down. You may need to follow the drawings for the first few times you do this exercise, but in time you will easily remember it, and it will simply become a part of your routine.

Now that you have created a twice daily routine for releasing stress, strengthening the nervous system and refining your energy, you have started the process for developing your creative and intuitive abilities. In the next chapter we will start working with the seven steps in the creative process.

The Seven Steps in the Creative Process

The mind is eternal in so far as it conceives things under
the form of eternity. . . . From this kind of knowledge
arrives the highest possible peace of mind, that is to say,
the highest joy, attended moreover, with the idea of
one's self.—Benedict Spinoza,
seventeenth century Dutch philosopher

In chapter 7 we introduced the seven steps in the creative process. It is now time for you to begin using them to create whatever you choose.

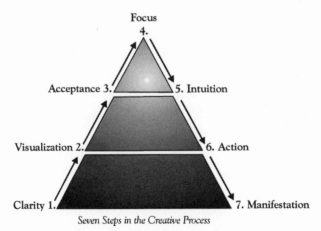

Seven Steps in the Creative Process

Step #1: Clarity

You will need a notebook for working with this process. You will be writing many very personal things in your notebook, so be sure to keep it in a private place. Start with a fresh sheet of paper and write a summary of where you are in your life right now. It is only for you, so be perfectly honest and describe as fully as you can all the different aspects of your life at the present time. When you have finished, put this paper in the back of your book. Later you can go back and read it and see how your life has changed as a result of working with this process.

Next take a clean sheet of paper and make a list of seven things that you like about your life. After you have finished this list, make another list of seven things that you *do not* like about your life.

Now you are ready to decide what you want to create for yourself. On another sheet of paper make a list of seven things that you want to create in your life. They can be anything that you desire. They can be concrete or abstract—the only requirement is that you will recognize it when you have created it.

Here are some examples of some things that you may want to create: personal habits or characteristics, inner peace, a special relationship, a fulfilling career, material things such as an automobile, a boat or a house. You get the idea; it can be anything you want in your life. The first place to start is to review the things you have in your life that you *do not* like. You may want to change these things.

We start with a list of seven because that is about as many as you can focus your attention on at one time. As you create these choices, you can cross them off your list and add others.

Remember, you are now beginning to create your life the way you want it to be. So the first question you need to ask yourself is, "What do I want?" Write your list now.

After you have finished your list, go back and look at it again, and ask yourself, "If I had this today, could I accept it?" If that works out, go back and start each item with "I choose." Remember you are making a *choice* to create these things in your life. Making a choice is making a commitment, and the subconscious needs to clearly understand that you are committed to creating these things. Do not say "I want." This is a very passive statement, and you can want something forever.

Here are some guidelines for making your choices:

1. Write the result you choose to create, not how you think it can be created. Focus your attention on what you want, not how you are going to get it.
2. Write in the present tense, as if it already exists.
3. Be sure to write what you want, not what you do not want.
4. Do not write what you think you should want. If reading it does not excite you, there is something wrong.
5. Do not make choices for other people. For instance, you can choose the kind of relationship you want, but don't name the other person in that relationship.

Go back over your choices and be sure they follow these guidelines. For instance, if you made a choice that reads something like this, "I choose to make a good impression at work so I will get a promotion," that violates guideline #1. You would want to change that choice to read something like this: "I choose to create a position for myself that I love, which gives me an opportunity to express myself and pays $___(name the amount) which I am worth and deserve." The main point here is to get as clear as possible about what you want and describe the result you want. Do not give a second thought as to how it will happen. Universal Intelligence will know how to create it. Your job is just to get clear about what you want and know that you can and will create it. How you will create it will be revealed to you as you go along.

A statement such as, "I choose to take a nice vacation sometime soon," violates guideline #2. Write in the present tense. First, it is not clear what you want and, next, it is not written in the present tense. You would want to change this choice to read something like this: "I choose a vacation in the Virgin Islands."

An example of a choice that violates guideline #3 would be something like this: "I choose to lose weight," or "I choose to get out of debt." Here you are focusing on what you do not want, excess weight and debt. These choices will need to be changed to, "I choose to create a healthy, lean, firm, beautiful body for myself," or "I choose to create the money I need to pay for all the things I choose to have in my life."

Do not use these examples as your choices. Your choices need to be exactly what you want. These are just examples to help you understand how to work with the guidelines. Next, let's look at #4. If you have a choice such as, "I choose to get a job that will please my mother," again you need to ask yourself, "What do I want?" You have no control over what others like or dislike. Your job is to create your life the way you want it to be. The idea is to get clear about what *you* want.

A violation of #5 would be a choice such as this: "I choose to have Bill/Susan fall in love with me." You get to make all of the choices about your life, but so does everyone else. Bill/Susan gets to choose who he/she falls in love with. When you understand that you are in charge of your own life, you will begin to see that we do not need to make choices for others. You can choose the kind of relationship you want, so you could change that choice to something like this: "I choose to have an intimate relationship with someone I love and who loves me."

We have been working with this process for many years, and thousands of people have taken our course. It is amazing to see what happens when people actually apply these principles in their lives. In one class a lady who was in a marriage that was not to her liking, asked if there was any way she could change her husband. My answer was, "You can only make choices for yourself," at which point she replied, "OK, I am going to create the kind of relationship I want whether it is with him or not." She then created her vision of the kind of relationship she wanted. In a few weeks she reported that she could not believe how her husband has changed. She said, "He is turning into my ideal mate." Did he change or did she change? I don't know. I can only tell you that Universal Intelligence brings us whatever perfectly fits our deepest beliefs and expectations. This is why it is extremely important to get as clear as possible about what we want in our lives.

You now have a list of seven things that you want to create for yourself and they are written according to the guidelines. We will now make two different kinds of choices. The seven choices you have already made we will call your main choices.

Now I want you to make five choices which we will call your basic choices. These are the choices we need to make to enable us to be able to create our main choices. These choices are so basic, you might have covered some or all of them in your main choices. If so you will now have room for some more main choices.

Basic choice #1 is to choose to love yourself. What does it mean to love yourself? Give this some thought. One of the things that comes to mind for me is to take care of myself. My understanding is that Love is who we are, so maybe it is taking the time to really get to know yourself. What you want to find out here is what this means to you. Take the time you need to get clear on this for yourself.

Basic choice #2 is to choose to choose, i.e., to choose to take charge of your life and create it the way you want it to be. Again you need to take the time necessary to decide what this means to you.

Basic choice #3 is to choose health: physical, mental, emotional and spiritual health. If you were totally healthy in all areas of your life what would that be like?

Things that come to mind for me on the level of physical health is feeling fully alive, full of energy and vitality. Every cell in the body is vibrant and intelligently playing its role in the proper functioning of the entire body. Mental health might mean being clear and sharp, alert and knowledgeable. Emotional health could mean feeling stable, secure, loved and loving, able to laugh and cry and experience all aspects of life. My definition of spiritual health could be feeling whole and complete, connected with my source, knowing that I am not separate, but at one with all. It could be being aware of the love and power that resides within me. These are just some thoughts on health, and how it might appear. Take some time and find out by asking yourself what it would mean to you to be healthy in all of the above areas. If you are choosing to be healthy, you will need to recognize it when you have created it.

Basic choice #4 is to choose freedom. What does it mean to be free? If you were totally free what would it feel like? Who keeps you from being free? Again take the time you need to discover what this means to you. Many times we believe that others keep us from being free. We now know that it is we ourselves who make all the choices in our lives. If you are feeling less than free in any area of your life you might want to consider making some different choices. Again, remember that this whole process is about taking charge of your life and creating it the way you want it to be.

Basic choice #5 is to choose to be true to yourself. What does it mean to be true to yourself? One of the things that comes to mind for me is to refuse to do anything that conflicts with my values. Does being true to yourself have anything to do with honesty? First, we want to be totally honest with ourselves, and when we are, we can be totally honest with others. Again, begin with this choice and see what it means to you.

Once you have worked through these five choices put them at the top of your list of choices. Creating these five choices makes it possible for us to create our other choices.

You now have all of your choices in place in your notebook. You will be working with these choices every day. You need to read your choices every morning, and every evening you will want to spend some time with them. Refine and update your choices as new insight comes to you. As we become more and more aware of what is truly important to us, many times our choices change. Remember, they are not set in stone. They can be changed. Sometimes people change their entire list, but most often they simply get new insights into how to best state their choices. When you work with your choices every day you will certainly get new insights about them, and you will get clearer about what you really want in your life.

What you will soon see as you continue to work with this process is that your choices will begin to be manifested. You will get whatever you have chosen, so you want to be sure it is exactly what you want. Remember, everything is energy and we are working with the law of attraction and repulsion to attract the energy necessary to create whatever we have chosen, and repel other energy that is undesirable to us.

Step #2: Visualization

The next thing we need to do is visualize what we want to create. Visualization is very easy. We all do it all the time. If I say "Think of a pink elephant," what happens in your mind? Usually, you automatically visualize a pink elephant. You create a mental picture of a pink elephant. In fact, it is almost impossible not to do it. When we create a vision or a picture in our mind it creates a form. The law of attraction will then pull the energy, necessary to fill this form, into our lives. Fortunately, this doesn't happen instantaneously, but as we live with a vision we intend to have manifested, the law of attraction begins to work. Our intention plays a major role in this process. This is why we preface each of our choices with "I choose," as an indication of intention or commitment.

Let's begin this process by picking a practice choice. Choose one of your choices to begin working with. Now in your mind's eye create a picture of something you would see if your vision were manifested. This does not have to be a still picture; it could be like a video clip.

Use as many of your senses as possible in creating this vision. For example, let's assume you want to create a new car for yourself. First it would be beneficial to go to a car dealership and look at the kind of car you want. Here you are impressing all of its features in your mind. In creating your vision, see the kind of car you want; see the emblem, see the body and the interior, and be sure to see the colors you want. A new car has a special new car smell. Smell the new car smell. Feel the steering wheel in your hands, and feel the kind of ride it delivers. Hear the wheels sing as they touch the pavement. The idea is to create the experience of having your new car. In your mind it is yours. Then very soon that mental picture will become physical due to how several of the laws of nature work. One of the laws is that mental energy directs physical energy.

Now create another picture of something that you will see when your vision is manifested. You might see yourself showing your new car to a friend. Again use as many senses as possible in creating this vision.

Now create a third picture of something that you will see when your vision is manifested. The idea here is to make your choice a part of your life on the mental level. It is just amazing to see how circumstances and events change to bring your visions into material manifestations when you create a clear vision of them.

Here is an example of how you might work with a different choice. Let's assume your choice is to create a life partner for yourself. What does he/she look like? Envision his/her personality. Imagine how he/she feels about you. Include everything that is important to you in this vision of the ideal mate you are creating for yourself. See the two of you together. What are you doing? If anything shows up in your mind that you do not want, immediately discard it and replace it with what you do want in this person. See, hear, feel, taste and smell this ideal partner and your relationship with him/her.

You will want to take some time to create at least three visions of each of your choices. Do not rush. You should be able to sense when each choice has become a part of your intention and expectation.

Step #3: Acceptance

Acceptance. That should be easy, right? Actually this is the most difficult step for most of us. This is where our beliefs come in. Do we not all believe that we can have whatever we want? We can have only what we can accept. The tricky part here is that we are not consciously aware of about eighty-five percent of what we believe. So the first step here is to become consciously aware of our beliefs.

Take a clean sheet of paper from your notebook and make a list of anything that comes to mind that could possibly keep you from creating your choices.

We have all had a tremendous amount of programing about how things work and what's possible. Remember that **beliefs are only information that we have accepted as truth,** but we are usually very attached to our beliefs. The scary part is that most of what is generally accepted as truth is not true, and most of us need to change most of our beliefs. There is no absolute truth except the laws of nature. If it is not a law of nature it is not necessarily true. Something can be true in one set of circumstances, but not true in another. This is relative truth. We very often believe that relative truth is absolute. We believe that if something is true in one situation it will also be true in another. This allows us to get through life without much need for thinking.

Now take your list of beliefs, which will all be of a negative nature, and change them to a positive belief, one that will coincide with the laws of nature we have been working with.

Here are some examples of things that most of us have programed into our psyches:

1. Money doesn't grow on trees—meaning that you do not have enough money for what you want, and you never will.
2. There are limits to what you can accomplish.
3. You must choose between financial success and personal freedom. You can't have everything.
4. Success is the result of hard work.

Are these statements true? No. They are all false. Just because money doesn't grow on trees it doesn't mean that you do not or will not have as much money as you need. Money is energy, and thought directs energy. We create lack in our lives only when we believe in it. Now let's look at #2. What determines the limits of your accomplishments? Your own thoughts create these limits. Now consider #3. Can you have financial success and personal freedom? Of course. You only need to choose both. Think about #4. What precedes action? Success is actually the result of clear thinking. You may need to do something. Activity is an important part of life, but remember that action follows thought. In order to be successful in anything, we first need to get in touch with our beliefs, and change them if they are not helping us to fulfill our choices.

Take all the time you need to work with this exercise. It is vitally important to get in touch with your beliefs. We cannot change beliefs until we are aware of them. Beliefs can only be changed on the conscious level of consciousness.

Go back over the summary of your life and the list of things that you have in your life that you do not like having. Ask yourself what beliefs you are holding that create these experiences in your life. Your life is, in fact, a perfect expression of your beliefs.

Make a list of all the things that could be causing you to create things that you do not want in your life. Now take all of your lists of beliefs and write the truth about them as we did in the examples. Remember, beliefs are only information that you have accepted as truth.

Now we want to work with a technique which we call "Reject, Reverse, Replace." Any belief that you discover that is not beneficial in helping you to create what you want, reject it. Tell yourself that this belief is not true, and you will not continue to believe it. Reverse the direction in which this belief has been taking you, and replace it with the truth about this situation. Create a new belief that supports you in your growth and success. It is only information. Accept only positive information that helps you to create what you want. Remember that you are an expression of Love, Intelligence and Energy. You are an integral part of a perfect system. What we are discovering here is how to live in harmony with this perfect system.

Becoming aware of our beliefs is a constant and continual process of observation, but once we have made the commitment to observe our thoughts it will be amazing to see how our beliefs show up. It is our thoughts and beliefs that are creating our experiences. Through the law of attraction and repulsion these beliefs are providing us with an exact replica of whatever we believe. As we change our limiting beliefs, we will see our experiences change to match.

Next let's take a look at what your beliefs are about yourself. Many people in our lives, beginning with our parents, have had opinions about us, and they usually openly related those opinions to us. We have either accepted or rejected their opinions, and that has determined to a great degree how we see ourselves. These opinions have either aided or undermined our self-esteem.

Now think back over your life and bring to mind what the people in your life have said to you about who you are, your abilities or lack of abilities. Write these all down. Now change them to be what you want to create for yourself. We now want to create an ideal self-image. Close your eyes and see yourself being the person you are choosing to be. Now say your name, and every time you close your eyes and say your name, become this ideal person.

Now you can see why the acceptance step is the most difficult for most people. It requires time, probably the rest of our lives, to be able to accept the lives we want for ourselves. However, when we continue to work with these techniques on a daily basis, we continue to make progress and create better and better lives for ourselves.

Another major aspect that we want to understand is that our beliefs are a part of the electromagnetic energy field which makes up our mind/body system. As we continue to do our stretching and breathing exercises, and meditate on a daily basis, the stress and negative energy is released from the mind/body system. This allows us to automatically become more confident and be able to change our beliefs to more positive, life supporting beliefs. We also are automatically expanding our awareness and becoming more aware of the laws of nature and how life works on all levels. Changing our beliefs without this healing, strengthening process is almost impossible. As our energy becomes more refined, our ability to see things from a different perspective increases.

Step #4: Focus

The experiences we bring into our lives are whatever we focus our attention on. In fact nothing exists for you until you focus your attention on it or acknowledge it. Attention brings energy to the object of our attention, which allows us to experience it. Since few people understand how this principle works, much is lost due to a lack of attention.

The following is an example of this principle. When I met my husband, he was looking for a position in the business world. He had worked in his family business and had been in private practice, but he had never actually applied for a job. He had a huge résumé with much impressive data, but when I asked him what he wanted to do, he didn't actually know. He said I could do this, this and this, naming about ten different possibilities. I explained this principle to him and showed him how he could not give any of these possibilities enough energy to allow them to manifest unless he got clear on what he wanted and focused his attention on that one choice. And, as you remember, he created a vision of what he would do if he had the opportunity to do what he wanted. He then manifested that vision. Part of the process was focusing his attention on his vision every day.

Another example is a very bright, energetic woman I knew. She was obviously very talented, and was involved in a number of different ventures. In fact, she seemed to be trying to go many different ways at the same time. However, none of her ventures paid off for her. How could it be that she was so busy, and had so many different possibilities, but nothing actually worked for her? It wasn't a lack of talent or ability. It was a lack of focus. Her energy was splintered, and she was not focusing enough energy in any one direction to bring it into being.

Understanding this principle helps us to realize the power we have in our own lives. If we focus enough attention on something, it will surely manifest in our lives. On the other hand, if we ignore anything it will disappear from our lives.

What we want to do is to reserve a block of time for focusing our attention on our choices. This is the reason why we work with only seven choices at a time. That is about as many things as we can give sufficient attention to in order to bring them into being. This is how we create.

Go back and look at your choices. Many times when we work with them for awhile, we realize that we can combine some of our choices, and actually make our list smaller. This is good. The smaller the list the more attention you can give to each one. In fact, it could be helpful to work with only two or three choices at a time. Select the ones that are most important to you and start there. Remember, you can mark them off once you have created them, and you can also add others.

I recommend working with (focusing your attention on) your choices twice a day. Once can be just to bring them into your awareness. The second time will require more time. Read them over first and notice if you have any new insights about them, such as how important they are to you, or if they are stated as clearly as you can get them, following the guidelines given for making your choices. Next expand on your choice. Write in as much detail as you can see. You will actually want to have two lists of choices, one that is written as succinctly as possible for a quick shot of attention (energy). The other should be written in as much detail as you can imagine.

Next you want to visualize the manifestation of your choice in three different pictures. This is focusing your attention on your choice and giving it energy.

After completing this, notice whether you have any resistance to accepting the full manifestation of your choice. Are there any negative thoughts that crop up? If so, work through the process for changing beliefs.

As you focus on your choices every day, you will soon notice circumstances and events occurring to help bring your choices into fruition.

Step # 5: Intuition

This is where our listening skills come into play. Most of us do not know how to listen. We get so caught up with what is going on in our lives that we have a hard time hearing what other people are saying to us. We always have something important to say. Have you ever caught yourself interrupting someone who is talking in order to express your opinion, or anxiously awaiting your turn to talk to the point of not actually hearing what the other person is saying? If we can't even listen to others, how can we hope to hear the very subtle voice of intuition?

Our inability to listen is a result of an overstressed nervous system. As we release the stress built up in the nervous system through the practice of the stretching exercises, breathing exercises, and meditation, we become more settled. A feeling of calmness and peace begins to emerge. We feel less pressure to talk, and begin to learn how to listen. As we continue to work with this process on a daily basis our ability to listen increases, and soon we begin to hear the inner voice of intuition.

Observation is the perfect tool to help us measure our progress. Do you still find yourself pushing to get your opinion into the conversation? When someone disagrees with you do you actually hear their point and consider it before replying?

When we have released enough stress, which keeps the mind/body energy heavy, the energy becomes more refined and intuition is an automatic result. We must become settled, quiet and peaceful in order to connect with clear intuitive awareness.

Intuition, like everything else, comes to us when we focus our attention on it. So let's start by thinking of a question. It should be a question that is important to you. It should require more than a yes or no answer. Write your question on a clean sheet of paper in your workbook.

Now close your eyes and use one of the forms of meditation that we learned in the chapter on meditation for a few minutes; then let go of the meditation technique, and ask your question. Open your eyes and write down the first thing that comes to you after asking your question. If it doesn't make any sense, write it down anyway. Try the same process again the next day.

Some people start with getting pieces of the answer they are seeking, and when they write down the answer they get each day, sometimes it begins to come together and make sense to them.

This process is just to teach the mind/body system that you are open to intuitive guidance, and you expect to get it. What happens after practicing the stretching, breathing and meditation techniques for a period of time is that you simply begin to know. Intuition becomes a part of your life, and questions are no longer necessary. You will begin to automatically know whatever you need to know, and your life becomes one of right action which brings about the desired results.

Distinguishing Between Intuition and the Intellect

Intuition is very different from a thought or belief. Intuition is simply a knowingness. It is very difficult to describe, and we must experience it for ourselves to truly understand it, but I want to give you some guidelines for distinguishing the difference.

A woman in one of my classes called me and was very upset. She thought she had received something intuitively that frightened her. First we need to understand that intuition is not attached to any emotion. If you get something that is frightening, that is coming from the intellect. Intuition comes from the level of wholeness. Anything of a negative nature is simply the absence of the awareness of the wholeness.

Intuitive awareness is not a thought, it is just awareness. We simply know something, and we have no doubt about it. We simply know that we know. It does not come from any logical determination. If someone asks, "How do you know?" we cannot explain it. Intuitive awareness just comes to us. My experience is that we receive intuitive awareness about things that are very important to us. When I ask a question I usually get an answer, but sometimes I do not get an answer. This to me means that I really do not need to know, that there is a reason for me to discover the answer in another way or that it will come when the time is right. Intuitive awareness is always there for us, but we must learn how to become quiet and still and tune into it.

Step # 6: Action

Once we become intuitively aware of what we need to do, we simply follow through with the appropriate action.

Action is easier for us because it is an outer process, and we are familiar with it. We are constantly doing things because this is the only way we know how to fulfill our desires if we are not familiar with the fourth dimension or spiritual dimension of ourselves. Now that we have become aware of how the entire creative process works we see action from a different perspective. It is simply a follow-through process after we have completed the five previous steps. Many of the problems we face are because we are so into action that we don't take the time away from it to discover what action needs to be taken and why. Without the five previous steps, action only depletes our energy and leaves us frustrated.

After getting very clear about what you want to create, visualizing it as complete and perfect, accepting it fully and asking for intuitive guidance for your action step, it is time to follow through with the appropriate action.

We must be willing to do our part. What is done for us is usually done through us. Universal intelligence will guide us once we have developed our ability to receive it. Then we act on the guidance we receive. Many times we will not be able to see why we are guided in a certain direction, but once we have learned to trust our intuitive awareness, we go with it. Then in time it will all unfold for us and we will be able to see it clearly.

Action is the last step which leads us to:

Step # 7: Manifestation

Actually manifestation is more of an occurrence than a step in the process. We add it as a step because we need to pay special attention to how the process works. When we work through the first six steps, manifestation is the result. We manifest whatever we have chosen to create.

Since this process works over time, the intellect sometimes has a hard time following it. Therefore, the manifestation step is to become aware of how the entire process works. By the time our visions are manifested we have totally accepted them, and if we are not observant we can think of them as just another experience and not realize how this experience came to be.

The manifestation step is for appreciation, joy and gratitude for the ability we have to create the lives we want for ourselves. It is to become aware of the process so we are prepared for our next creation.

My New **18** Lifestyle

*If we live truly, we shall see truly. It is as easy for the
strong to be strong as it is for the weak to be weak. When
we have new perception, we shall gladly disburden the
memory of its hoarded treasures.*—Ralph Waldo Emerson

Morning Routine

Wake up after approximately eight hours of sleep. After your
bathroom trip, which includes brushing teeth, go outside, or at
least get your head outside into the fresh air, and do three purifying breaths. A purifying breath is a deep breath through the
nose, bringing the air all the way down to the abdomen and
filling the chest, then forcefully exhaling through the mouth.
This fills the lungs with fresh air and releases the stale air that
may have accumulated in the lungs overnight. Do this only three
times.

Spread your special exercise blanket in your designated
place for doing your program, sit in the center of it and start
your massage toward the heart. Continue with the full set of
energizers.

Upon completion of the energizers, sit in a comfortable,
crossed-leg position or in a chair with your back straight and
supported. Then do your balanced breath exercise for two minutes. Have a clock where you can see it. Now close your eyes
and meditate for twenty minutes.

After meditation bring to consciousness one of your choices and visualize it as fully accomplished. Then open your eyes and read through your full list of choices.

Evening routine

Do your full set of stretching energizers, or, if time is a factor, do the short version at the end of chapter sixteen. Meditate for twenty minutes, then before opening your eyes ask a question for which you want an answer (see chapter 17 on how to work with questions) or visualize the full manifestation of one of your choices.

Sometime before bed, take at least thirty minutes and read over your list of choices, visualize them and update them as new insights come to you.

Things to observe and make choices about in your daily life

If we do not learn how to be conscious about the things that are happening in our lives, we simply react to our programing and function like robots. When we do this we give away our power to consciously create whatever we want. We have all been well programed about what is "supposed" to be. We know what a woman is supposed to be like, and what a man is supposed to be like. We know what a good wife and husband are supposed to be like. What good parents are like. What children are supposed to do, think, be. We know what friends and neighbors are supposed to do. We know how to run a business and the government. We have beliefs about everything in our lives. What we are usually unaware of is how we came to these beliefs. Most of them have been programed into our thinking from other people, including the media. Many times these people have a vested interest in what we believe. Most of the things we believe have never been consciously considered by us. It is now time to get conscious, and start making choices for ourselves.

When something upsets you, ask yourself which of your beliefs is being threatened. Consider whether this belief is helping you to create what you want in your life. Ask how important it is to you. When we get upset we damage our health. Is this really important enough for you to want to damage your health?

Notice what you think and say. Is it in accord with what you want to create in your life?

When you catch yourself condemning, complaining or criticizing someone or something, including yourself, ask yourself if this has any value. Will this help create the life you want? Remember the law of attraction—what comes from us returns to us.

Observe your body. Is it relaxed? Is your mind focused on what you are doing?

Notice how you are affected by the people in your life. If many of the people in your life are negative and leave you feeling drained after being with them, you might want to find some new friends. It is a good rule of thumb to associate with people who have as much life force as you do or more.

Notice how you are affected by the entertainment that you engage in. When you see a movie or TV show, or when you read a book, magazine or newspaper, for all practical purposes you are experiencing whatever you are focusing your attention on. Are these the kind of experiences that you really want in your life?

Observe how stress affects the people around you. We can see stress causing people to behave in ways that would not occur if they were not overstressed. Notice the stress in your life and how it affects your behavior.

Observe how much of your life is your present experience. When we are thinking about the past or the future, we are missing the present. Life is now; we can only live in the present.

Notice if you find yourself rehashing old events or conversations. One of the most valuable things that we can learn is that when something is over it is *over*. There is nothing more that we can do about it. It is now a part of the past. We need to let it go and move on with our lives.

Are you willing to experience whatever is? We can spend days, weeks, even years, dreading something that we fear might happen. The minute you decide to experience whatever is, you are freed. A great technique to practice is to consciously let go of our resistances and experience whatever is. What you will find is that your thoughts about something and the experience will be quite different.

Notice how well you receive. It is our beliefs that block our ability to receive. Become a master receiver.

Practice using your ideal self-image technique on a regular basis. Simply say your name to yourself and become the ideal self that you created earlier.

Observe your diet. Do you overeat or drink? Is your food fresh? How do you feel after eating? Observe the role of exercise in your life. Do you exercise on a regular basis? Walking in the fresh air at least thirty minutes a day can be very helpful.

Here are some important things to do after you have been practicing the stretching exercises, breath exercises, meditation and observation techniques for at least three months:

Go back to the summary that you wrote describing your life when you began this process. How much has your life changed? We do this exercise in our classes, and most people find dramatic changes have taken place. I remember one woman who said "I do not even know this person that I have written about any more."

If you feel you need to more clearly understand your purpose in life, ask to know your purpose after your meditation before opening your eyes. Ask this as you would ask any other question and work with it in the same way. Write down whatever comes to you and keep asking the question until you feel that you are clear about the answer.

Now take some time, as much as you need, to think about the life you would like to create for yourself. Write the story of your life. You can write in the third person if that is easier. Make it just the way you want it to be. Now visualize that life unfolding for you, and accept it. Make a commitment to yourself to create this life. Now work with the seven steps in the creative process to create your life just the way you want it to be.

Our creations always go through a process. The first part of the process is when we create our visions. This is fun and we are very excited; but then comes the germination phase. This is the unseen part. It is like planting a seed. We cannot see any-thing happening for what seems like a long time, but then the plant begins to sprout. The same is true with our creations. There is a time when our visions are taking root, when all the things that are necessary to manifest our visions are taking place, but we cannot see them. This is a time for patience and not a time for doubt. If we doubt, it is like digging up the seed to see what is happening. This would disturb the rooting process and you would have to start all over. No one knows how long it will take for our visions to manifest, but just as surely as the seed we put in the ground will produce a plant if we keep it watered, so will our visions manifest. We only need to keep them watered by keeping our attention focused on them and being willing to do our part.

If you follow this routine on a daily basis it will lead you through a transformation process which leads to self-actualization. In the next chapter we will see how this process unfolds.

Transformation 19

Of all knowledge, the wise and good seek most to know
themselves.—William Shakespeare

Just as the caterpillar must go through a transition or metamorphosis to become a butterfly, we must also go through a
transformation to become self-actualized.

In our caterpillar state, or in the state of ordinary consciousness, we have only the use of the conscious and the subconscious mind. We are limited to the information provided
by the five senses. In this state our life consists of memory, beliefs, judgment, ego, personality, objective thinking and problems. We can live our whole lives on this level if we choose.

However, it is a choice. Just like the caterpillar we can choose
to go through our own metamorphosis. When we choose to
do the program laid out in this section on a daily basis, changes
start to take place. The mind/body energy is refined, enabling
us to release the stress stored in the nervous system and merge
the conscious mind with the superconscious. This strengthening of the system allows us to expand our awareness and change
our beliefs or programing, thereby making it possible for us to
create proper functioning throughout the entire mind/body
system. This new way of functioning refines the energy of the
entire system so it begins to resonate with the energy of the
superconscious. As you remember, the superconscious is the
level of all knowledge, the source of intuition.

Choosing to go through this transformation brings us to self-actualization. As a self-actualized person we enjoy intuitive guidance in all that we do. Our daily lifestyle brings us in contact with universal intelligence, all knowledge and love, and our everyday realization of our oneness with all. Some of the results that we usually experience are optimal health, happiness, joy, enthusiasm, compassion, success and wealth—spiritual, cultural and material.

In most cases we also get a clear sense of purpose. We all have a shared purpose, which is to grow into self-actualization and mastery. Then we each have a special gift to share with the world around us. When we are in touch with this purpose and are living our lives on purpose, we feel totally fulfilled. Your purpose need not be something that appears to be spectacular, but it is important and only you can fill that purpose.

Every one of us can choose this new lifestyle and create a much expanded life for ourselves.

How might this new way of functioning unfold in your life?

I could write another book on the experiences of people who have participated in our classes and how it changed their lives. People have healed themselves of heart problems, cancer and numerous other ailments. They have also created new businesses, and lives that are far more fulfilling than they could have ever imagined. Your experiences will depend on what you want and your level of discipline in following the guidelines. However, what I want to do here is to give you an example of how using this process works.

With her permission, I would like to share with you some of the experiences Joan Gustafson has had as a result of this program.

Joan was introduced to our Unlimited Futures course by a fellow executive at 3M. He shared with Joan the many benefits he had gained from the course in both his personal life and in his ability to make his contribution to 3M.

Joan came to the course with three major goals in mind. First, she wanted to create a compatible, loving partner with whom to share her life. Second, she wanted to build her dream house. And third, she wanted to expand her responsibilities and influence within 3M.

She had been dating Cliff for several months, but the relationship didn't seem to be going anywhere. Cliff came to the introductory session with her, and he decided to take the course also. As it turns out, Cliff had had a heart attack, and Joan was very worried about a possible recurrence. They both learned the power of thoughts, and they both began to see Cliff as perfectly healthy. This removed Joan's fear, which was creating a gulf between them. Cliff's health improved, their relationship grew stronger, and they were married the next year.

She had her house up for sale when she came to the course, but it wasn't selling. She had found the place where she wanted to build her dream house, but she couldn't do that until her present house was sold. She begin visualizing the house selling and the new house being built. She visualized this in detail, and within a few weeks a cash offer came in on her house. She moved into an apartment and began building her dream house on the lovely pond she had found.

She also decided what she would like to do at work. She created a vision of a new department that she would create for 3M. Before the three-month class was completed, she had been offered the opportunity to do exactly what she had created in her mind. She was able to select the people for this new department, and she chose wisely. It was a great group of people. One of the first things she wanted to do was introduce her new department to our executive development program. We held a half-day workshop for them, and at the end of the session we told them about the executive development program. She asked them if they would like to participate in it. Before the day was over they had all responded in the affirmative. She included her boss in this session, who also chose to participate in the continuing course.

Our executive development program is provided in four two-day sessions held once a month in a special conference center. She had ten managers in her new department which was the perfect size for our program. They all came and experienced outstanding results. They have all made great contributions to 3M, and have created much more fulfilling lives for themselves.

Joan's next goal was to create an international position for herself. She had decided that she wanted to expand her new department to Europe. She was told that international assignments were almost nonexistent at the time. This, of course, didn't faze Joan. She knew how thought and visualization works, so she simply stayed focused on her vision, following the seven steps in the creative process, and within a short time the opportunity she had envisioned appeared.

Cliff was a chiropractic doctor, and he was able to sell his practice in the exact time frame they needed to make the move. They were in Europe, based in Paris, with a beautiful house in the countryside for two years. Joan traveled all around Europe working with the different 3M offices, and Cliff came along. She accomplished her business objectives and they had a great time during their two years in Europe, just as Joan had envisioned.

Joan has now taken early retirement from 3M and has written *A Woman Can Do That!: Ten Strategies for Creating Success in Your Life,* a book designed to help women become more successful in the business world. She and Cliff have built a beautiful new house in Arizona for their semiretirement. Joan has started her own business, which will provide seminars and workshops. Her new company is "Success and Leadership Dynamics." Her slogan is "Opening doors to brighter futures for individuals and organizations."

As a result of practicing the program laid out in this section Joan has taken charge of her life and is creating it just the way she wants it.

You also have dreams, and you can make them come true by developing your ability to take charge of your life and creating it just the way you want it to be.

High Tech/High Touch

Go back into yourself. Truth dwells in the inner man.
—St. Augustine

Technology has moved us into a whole new world. We can know and do things that we never dreamed possible in the past. It also demands that we evolve with it. Just as every major discovery in the past has made our past abilities obsolete, so has the world of technology. Once we discovered how to make matches, our ability to rub rocks together to start a fire became obsolete. We no longer need to remember our multiplication tables, since we all have calculators to do that for us.

Things are moving faster and faster, and we must make immediate decisions. There is no time for analysis anymore. Then how do we make our decisions?

Life and decision-making get harder and harder every day for the ordinary person. This causes stress, and the stress mounts. When the nervous system becomes overstressed, that affects our perception, which causes us to make mistakes. Mistakes cause more stress, and all of life can seem to move into a downward cycle. If we are doctors, nurses, pharmacists or pilots, our mistakes can cost lives. For most of us our mistakes are less costly, but nevertheless costly.

What can be done about it? When we choose a lifestyle that focuses our attention on releasing the stress that builds up in the nervous system on a daily basis the system becomes stronger. A strong nervous system provides clarity in perception, which helps us to achieve our goals. Achieving our goals makes us even stronger, and we begin to create an upward spiral in our ability to create better lives for ourselves.

We must develop our intuition in order to function well in a high-tech world. We can now get more information in a split second than we could ever use. We must determine the value of the information we get, and what information will be helpful to us. The intellect alone cannot survive high tech. However, we can choose to develop our intuitive abilities which allows us to make immediate decisions which are in our best interest. Intuitively we can know. The intellect can only think or use reason and logic which is much too slow for the high-tech world in which we find ourselves.

What is important?

Recently, I read an article about several people who were now billionaires several times over. They were young and had made an enormous amount of money as a result of technology.

However, the article said they were all severely depressed and could find no meaning to life.

If you could be granted one request for your life, what would you ask for? Most of us would probably ask for happiness. Most of the things we do are in pursuit of happiness. Have we been looking in the wrong places for happiness?

The technology we now enjoy is a major evolutionary step for us as a society in an outer direction, where we have focused most of our attention. We have gained outer success, but what about what is most important to us.

Technology and everything in the outer world is only a means for us to use in our growth. It is the inner development that makes life really worthwhile.

The self-actualized person functions well in the outer world, because he knows both the inner and the outer world, and understands how they relate to each other. He understands what is important. He has conquered fear, which allows him to feel peaceful, whole and complete regardless of what appears to be happening in the outer world. He knows that the outer world can be changed from within himself.

The soft stuff (high touch) is actually where all the power lies. We usually think of high touch as our relationship with other people, which helps us to keep from getting lost in our relationship with all of the machines in our lives. Here we are relating it to our relationship with ourselves.

We have all the power we need right within ourselves to create our lives just the way we want them to be.

What kind of life will you create? It is all a matter of choice. I hope this book has given you the insight and techniques for creating the life you want.

The Unlimited Futures mission is to "provide programs and an environment which allows each of us to discover who we are, how we function, our purpose and how to accomplish it, thereby creating a network of people around the world who are creating the lives they want for themselves and are actively helping others to do the same."

Thank you for helping me fulfill my purpose.

Now please return to page one and reread this book. Every time you read it you will discover more about who you are, how you function and how to create the life you want for yourself.

Enjoy your daily routine and the wonderful life you are creating.

My Vision

My vision is to provide a facility where you could come to stay for awhile, to have a vacation where you could discover the spiritual essence that underlies all of the material world, right within yourself. It would be a place that would totally support you in creating a new lifestyle that would support your continued growth toward optimal health which includes self-actualization.

You can follow the guidelines in Part Four of this book, and do this on your own. However, it would be quicker and easier if you could take some time away so you could put your full attention to getting to know yourself, uncovering your beliefs, making some new choices, and laying the foundation for a new lifestyle. My vision is to provide a place where this would be possible for you.

I will share what I would like this facility to be like, so you can also help me to visualize it. I will also write it according to the guidelines that I gave you in Part Four for writing your choices or visions. One of the guidelines is to write in the present tense, as if it already existed.

This facility is located in a natural setting. There is water, and walking paths by the water and through the woods. It is secluded so you can relax completely and feel perfectly safe. It is a special place where you constantly enjoy the beauty of nature, and all the comforts of luxury living. The entire facility portrays a feeling of peace, serenity, affluence, comfort and beauty. The rooms are spacious with plush carpeting, queen size beds, adjoining baths, plenty of room for doing stretching exercises, a large comfortable chair for meditation and a nice desk for writing your choices and creating the vision for your new life. The rooms have lots of windows and a sliding glass door opening onto a lanai.

The dining room is an indoor/outdoor environment overlooking the water. Classrooms are spacious and comfortable allowing for at least ten people to do exercises as well as to sit comfortably for the other part of the sessions. In addition to the private rooms, dining room, classrooms and offices, there is a large room for large gatherings where we could have special celebrations, guest speakers, etc.

This facility provides a space where you could come to take charge of your life, lay the foundation for higher levels of health and development and a whole new way of functioning. This is a place for evaluating one's life and making the desired changes. It is a place for releasing the built-up stress in your mind and body, making new choices, and creating a new vision for yourself.

There are places for people to go who are sick, but this is a place for proactive people, healthy people who want to get healthier—successful people who want to be more successful or to enjoy their success more.

Every part of this facility provides for health. The food is fresh and mostly organic. We have our own gardens and grow the most highly energized fruits and vegetables possible. We also serve fresh fish, chicken and turkey. The food is served in an elegant and appealing manner. A juice bar is also provided where you can stop by for a glass of fresh fruit or vegetable juice or your favorite smoothie. The water is also of the highest standards, clean and clear.

Programs are designed for people staying anywhere from ten days to three months. It is also a place for our regular executive development programs. The programs are scheduled to provide for time alone, silence, exercise, walks in the woods and by the water, to enjoy our great food, experience great massages and classes for gaining greater knowledge and understanding.

This is the place for the greatest vacation of your life, a different kind of vacation, one that is truly revitalizing, one with a very special purpose. And, of course, you can return as often as you like.

Thanks for helping me visualize this special place. Let's see how long it takes us to manifest it. You can stay in touch by logging on to our web site at www.unlimitedfutures.org.

Index

About the Author

Bobbie R. Stevens, Ph.D., is cofounder and president of Unlimited Futures, LLC, an organization that has been providing programs for the development of human potential for more than twenty years. She holds doctorates in both psychology and business management. After a successful career in business, she moved into the field of industrial psychology, and in 1979 she founded the American Institute for Creativity, Health and Productivity. Dr. Stevens's work has resulted in a higher quality of life for thousands of individuals, and her executive development programs have made outstanding contributions to many fortune 500 companies as well as to numerous smaller companies. Dr. Stevens lives and works with her husband, Dr. Dean Portinga, in Naples, Florida.

More Information

For more information on the Unlimited Futures programs, to give us feedback or to subscribe to our newsletter, please visit our Web site at: www.unlimitedfutures.org.
You may e-mail us at: Unlimitedfutures@ATT.net
Call us at: 941-513-3804
or write: Unlimited Futures
               1083 N. Collier Blvd. #280
               Marco Island FL 34145

Book orders:
Large-quantity discounts are available to organizations or groups.
Contact:
               Tara Publishing
               3823 Tamiami Trail East, #232
               Naples, FL 34112
               Phone: 941-513-4029
Or, you may order via e-mail at TaraPublishing@ATT.net
or call toll free: 1-866-563-1493.